S0-CPS-184

WINDSOR CASTLE

BY

SIR OWEN MORSHEAD

PHAIDON

THEIR MAJESTIES IN GARTER ROBES

WINDSOR CASTLE

by

SIR OWEN MORSHEAD

Librarian to H.M. the King

LONDON · PHAIDON PRESS

1 Cromwell Place, London, S.W.7
1951

MADE IN GREAT BRITAIN
TEXT PRINTED BY WESTERN PRINTING SERVICES LTD. BRISTOL
PLATES PRINTED BY JARROLD AND SONS LTD. NORWICH

CONTENTS

The illustrations of Their Majesties The King and Queen are taken from photographs for which special sittings were granted to Mr. Harold White, F.I.B.P., F.R.P.S., by whom also the photographs of the castle were taken.

FOREWORD

IN *writing this book I have kept at my elbow* The Architectural History of Windsor Castle *by the late Sir William St. John Hope, which was published in two stately volumes in* 1913 *and remains the touchstone to which assertion and theory are brought for confirmation or dismissal. It contains no less than* 1,040 *passages in medieval Latin, transcribed by him from documents in the Public Record Office; and to these he compassionately supplied a translation and an index. I have not complicated the text of this essay by inserting references to the book from which the facts are quarried, but I would not fall short of the fullest acknowledgment of the debt which I owe it, nor fail to express from afar my admiration for the scholarship which it betokens.*

"Hope is a good breakfast," wrote Francis Bacon, "but a bad supper." Sir William was an archaeologist ; he lost interest after 1700, *and patience after* 1800. *For the later period I cannot claim his authority ; and indeed throughout the story I must absolve him from responsibility for the structure raised upon his foundations. I have tried to solve the problems which have formulated themselves in my own mind during the course of twenty-five years' residence in the castle, and to answer those questions which I have found to interest and perplex others. I have not darkened counsel by discussing topics which are no longer alive, such for instance as Denton's Commons and Crane's Buildings, of which no traces remain.*

I hope it will be evident how deep is the veneration in which I hold this house, and the gratitude which I owe to the King for allowing me to write about it. When first I came I had everything to learn, and Queen Mary to learn it from; and nothing could exceed the kindness which has been my unvarying lot. I found that this is not an extinct palace like Hampton Court or Kensington, but a living home with a domestic character and personality of its own, and a human quality investing its stones and mortar. This is easy to say; an illustration may make it more easily understood by those who see its apartments under the conditions of a museum.

One Easter bank holiday in such a year as 1930 *King George V was in the print room of the library, overlooking the North Terrace. Crowds passed and repassed below the window, and presently I fell to telling him the story about King George III, who had inhabited during the decade of his insanity the room in which we then were. His clouded mind used to take in little of the day's events, but on hearing the tread of soldiers on the terrace below he would stand at the window to see them pass. The command 'Eyes Right' would be given, and the King would raise his hand in acknowledgment. One day early in* 1820, *while the old King lay in his coffin, the Ensign on duty looked up out of habit as he passed beneath the window, and to his surprise saw the bearded figure in its accustomed posture. So confident was he that his eyes did not betray him that he gave the word of command—and received the customary response.*

"Yes," said the King when the story was done, "that is right. I know because the Ensign told me. He was old Sir William Knollys, Comptroller to my father when I was a boy. I was eighteen when he died."

The same evening after dinner I told this to Lord Colebrooke, who was then in waiting. "I know that room," he said. "It is the first room in the castle that I went into. I was taken in by my uncle, Lord Sydney, who began as Groom of the Bedchamber to King George IV and ended as Lord

Steward to Queen Victoria. My uncle used to tell me how when he was a boy at Eton he would visit his aunt, Miss Georgeana Townshend, who as Lady Housekeeper occupied Norman Tower, where the Deputy Governor lives to-day. If he had been good she would take him across into the castle; there, finger on lip, she would point to a door in the narrow passage just inside, and he would hear the demented old King moving within. If he were having a disturbed day he would be pacing up and down, and sometimes roaring: at other times the stillness would be broken by snatches of Handel as he groped in his darkness upon the keys of the harpsichord."

Thus in the ordinary round of daily life do the memories of yesterday melt into the traditions of to-day, cherished not only by the august family whose name is linked with the house, but by us servants too whose life and duty are bound up with it and them. Similar recollections are exchanged among the craftsmen who, often like their fathers before them, find here an outlet for their skills; and these stories, shared in the fellowship of a common devotion, make fast the hold which the castle exercises upon the minds and affections of all who make their business within its walls.

DOMINE DILEXI DECOREM DOMVS TVAE
ET LOCVM HABITATIONIS GLORIAE TVAE

Windsor Castle,
Easter 1951.

O. M.

Chapter I

THE NORMANS

THOSE who call Windsor home share the knowledge of a point some three miles to the south-west, where St. Leonard's Hill offers a view of such startling beauty that were it in any country but his own the Englishman would endure travel and hardship to see it. You round a bend in one of King George the Fourth's woodland rides, and on a sudden the castle is there, gleaming upon its knoll in the middle distance, couched like the swan upon her nest in the silvery Thames below: not isolated in space, nor stark and deserted like some crusader's castle amid Syrian sands, but lapped in the soft landscape of England, which rises behind it into the blue distance till earth and sky merge in a rimless infinity.

As in space, so too in time. Set in the middle distance, almost indeed the foregound, of the perspective of history, behind it rise layer upon layer of other scenes, and a babel of other tongues, in the unending recession which leads the mind back to ages beyond the record of man. Beside me on the table as I set out to trace its story lies a bronze coin turned up by the spade last year. It bears the head of the Emperor Domitian, he who recalled Agricola from his governorship of south Britain. Minted in the year 88, it emerges from a back garden in Windsor after almost 2000 years to remind us that Roman legionaries were garrisoning these parts while St. Luke was writing his gospel.

A glance at the map makes plain the wooded character of the countryside in the earliest days that we need to consider. Names such as Bearwood, Beech Hill, Oakingham (modernised as Wokingham) abound. There is Hurst, with Tilehurst and Sandhurst: there are the holts, such as Bagshot or badger's holt, and Aldershot, the holt of alders. Alternating with the woodlands we find the open glades or fields; without going far one could thread an alphabet of them, from Arborfield, Binfield and Burfield, to Swallowfield, Warfield and Winkfield. Two Englefields shew us where settlers from East Anglia infiltrated into this part of Wessex, and there is even a Danesfield to testify to the taming in our midst of a party of that marauding race.

Probably the inhabitants to-day of the county of Berkshire alone outnumber the Saxon population of the whole island, who therefore did not need to bring more than a small portion of the soil under their laborious husbandry. The forest provided a livelihood for their herds of swine; and these, when they were not grouting for roots and finding their own subsistence of beechmast and acorns, would be pastured upon winter leys—as the name Swinley in this neighbourhood reminds us.

These early settlements were no doubt linked by bridle paths and footpaths, but of roads as we know them there were in this part of the country few. Loads beyond the capacity of a packhorse could be dragged across country on sledges, but it was simpler to use water transport: and thus it is that the rivers assumed an importance far transcending that which we accord them to-day. In the minds of our generation they appear as decorative adjuncts to such places as Durham or Windsor, whereas these strongholds were so sited in order to challenge an enemy seeking the easier passage by water into the heart of the island. It was by Thames that the stone travelled down from the Cotswold quarries to build the colleges and abbeys beside its banks, from Oxford down to Reading and Eton; and it was up the Thames that the royal barges would bear the Court on their periodical visits to Windsor. By water Queen Elizabeth, then princess, came from the Tower of London to Windsor in 1554, breaking her journey at Richmond; and King Charles II used to make the journey by river as late as 1680.[1] Granted that the tides were more helpful before the modern locks were installed, it must seem at best a cumbersome mode of transport to us. We do well, however, to consider the alternative. "In the seventeenth century," wrote Macaulay, "the inhabitants of London were, for every practical purpose, further from Reading than they are now from Edinburgh. It happened almost every day that coaches stuck fast, until a team of cattle could be procured from some neighbouring farm to tug them out of the slough."

To-day at Windsor we apply the term Forest only to a narrow curving belt of woodland which forms the rind, as it were, to the Great Park; and together they measure some five miles from north to south, and less than three miles across. But in former times the royal domain was by a great deal larger, extending twenty miles southward to where the long ridge of the Hog's Back links Guildford with Farnham, and swinging westwards certainly as far as the river Loddon, which flows northwards into the Thames at about fifteen miles upstream from Windsor, on the outskirts of Reading. Always, however, it was bounded on the north by the Thames, where the king's house was situated for ease of access; and on the east by Runnymede, only three miles downstream, where King John met the barons in 1215 and signed Magna Charta.

That habitation of the Saxon kings was not the one which we associate with Windsor to-day. It was situated at the first point on the royal estate which the barges would have reached on their long grind up the river from London. The train of boats would pull in at Runnymede, whence the baggage would be carried to Bears Rails, just within the Great Park, about a mile from the river and on higher ground. In 1919 this site was excavated and the results are discussed in the *Illustrated London News* of 28 February 1920. Harwood (*Windsor Old and New*, page 58) favours another site, close to the river bank and adjoining the church: but it is common ground that the palace stood in the parish of Old Windsor, and that nothing remains of it to-day.

Such, then, was the condition of affairs prior to 1066. But William the Conqueror, having acquired his new kingdom by force, proceeded to consolidate his hold upon it; and he lost no time in establishing throughout the country a system of defensive strongholds, each capable of offering security not only to its own garrison but also to such of his adherents in its neighbourhood as might need protection. And first London, then as now the capital, though little larger than Windsor to-day. It had grown up where it is because that was the lowest point at which the Thames could be spanned

HIS MAJESTY THE KING

HER MAJESTY THE QUEEN

by a bridge; but this in itself might not have ensured its primacy had not other considerations, economic and geographical, combined to favour it. The statesman and the soldier in William were in accord in looking to its defence, the one being concerned to avert the rape of the seat of government, and the other having an eye to the roads which converged upon its bridge. Furthermore, although the Conqueror himself had chosen to launch his attack upon Hastings Gap, he could not be unaware that the joint estuary of the Medway and the Thames must offer a tempting gateway to others—as indeed it still did to the Dutch six centuries later. He therefore built that object so familiar to us, the Tower of London, downstream from London Bridge which it was designed to defend. From it the old London Wall, built by his forerunners, the Roman invaders, hemmed in the little town, which occupied the north bank of the river only; and where the Wall rejoined the river further upstream, about where the Temple stands to-day, he constructed another fortification called Baynard's Castle, which has since disappeared.

So much for the close defence of the capital. But no commander responsible for the security of a city confines all his troops within its curtilage, lest in the event of civil commotion they should be overwhelmed. Nowadays he may derive comfort from Belloc's couplet

> Whatever happens we have got
> The Maxim gun and they have not,

but in times which we call less civilised the scales were more evenly held, and a crack on the pate from a weaver's beam was equally discouraging to soldier and civilian alike. Prudence dictated the holding of reserves within a day's march, and we often find that capital cities have a garrison town near at hand. Thus Paris has its Versailles, Berlin its Potsdam—and London its Windsor, which still provides barracks for a regiment of horse and a battalion of footguards.

Whether or not he was actuated by such considerations as these, William the Conqueror clapped a ring of fortresses round his capital. If London be pictured as the centre of a clock dial, of which the hour hand is some 25 miles long, we find Berkhamsted at 11 o'clock, Hertford at 12, Ongar at 1 and Rayleigh at 2; and at each may be seen the remains of one of the four castles which screened London north of the river. Then at Rochester (3 o'clock), where the River Medway joins the Thames, he reared that stone tower which still dominates the confluence of the two waterways. At Tonbridge (5 o'clock) and on the North Downs at Reigate (at 6), there are others: and penultimately at Guildford (at 7), whose castle stands at the southern apex of the crown domain as it then was. He closed the ring with Windsor, at 9 o'clock; and this was to be the most important of them all, designed not only for mewing his falcons and kennelling his hounds, but to play its part in the peripheral defence of his capital, and in particular to command that river which formed the main thoroughfare of the kingdom. First in importance, it is the only one to remain.

In planning his Windsor fortress he abandoned the low-lying abode that had served his Saxon predecessors. With his keener eye he saw that by going three miles upstream he could secure the advantage of a hill overlooking the Thames, whose waters in primeval times had scoured its northern flank to a pitch so abrupt that a man can hardly scramble up it without dropping on hands and knees. Here, ready to hand, was a sound defensive position for an army of occupation; for entrenchment upon their new territory was the immediate policy of the Normans. The escarpment made the castle impregnable from the north (Plate 2), more especially in early days, when its walls rose sheer from the chalk hill. Later ages could afford to weaken its defences by the construction of the North Terrace, overlooking the Thames Valley (Plate 6). But, terrace or no terrace, the habitation of the king himself, from William the Conqueror to George III, was always on the sunless and chilly north flank: and this is no coincidence, for it was the safest place.

Except at Richmond the Thames is dominated by no comparable eminence between Windsor and London. It is a lonely outcrop of the Chiltern hills, commanding views disproportionate to its apparent consequence. The Ordnance Survey bench-mark upon its grassy summit records that its height above sea level is a mere 50 yards, or 157 feet to be exact, but Harrow and the Crystal Palace and Epsom Downs are visible; little but the trees of Fort Belvedere shut out the Hog's Back to which allusion has been made; to the west it is the high ground of the Chilterns near Shillingford Bridge that closes the view towards Oxford, while northwards the eye travels far out across the wide valley to the green-mantled hills of Buckinghamshire.

But it was not the long views that attracted the Conqueror. In the eleventh century it was of little use (except perhaps for lighting a beacon) to be able to see more than four or five miles. They had no telescopes and could not tell friend from foe; they disposed of diminutive forces, and these could consequently move under cover; the pace of war was sluggish; their weapons were of the shortest range, and once having chosen a defensive position there was little to be done but await the shock of encounter. What attracted the Normans, apart from the local command of vision, was something quite different: they knew when they were not wanted, and in facing an unfriendly populace they preferred to have the cliff at their back. Moreover, we must remember that until the day before yesterday war was a matter of display and defiance, not the stealthy traffic of khaki and camouflage to which it has fallen within our lifetime. From Minden to Tel-el-Kebir British troops wore scarlet and made themselves big with bearskins; and when they formed their bristling squares they chose the open plain. So it had been from earliest times. The fortress builders cast up their ramparts and formed their squares of stone in the most prominent positions, and cried like Goliath the Philistine, "Come to me, and I will give thy flesh unto the fowls of the air."

The name of the castle should not by rights have been Windsor at all. But it was with castles as it is in our own day with airfields; they were apt to be sited not among the busy haunts of men but upon lonely uplands, of which the local names sound strangely in our ears. Who, upon learning that the king was gone hunting in Windsor forest, would be likely to have heard of the adjacent village of Clewer? Yet it was in that parish that the new hilltop fortress technically lay, though popular usage did not acknowledge the fact. Officially it became known as New Windsor,[2] and indeed is so known to local government still; but it was inevitable that before long the tail should wag the dog, and for centuries now the Saxon village at the foot of the hill has had to content itself with the appellation Old Windsor.

When a child makes a castle on the seashore it will first trace a circle in the sand and then dig a ditch around it, throwing up the sand to form a mound in the middle. The ditch is dry until the tide approaches, but even dry it constitutes a formidable addition to the defences of the castle. A stick can be driven down through the heart of the mound and a well thus created, so that if the garrison is beset they can carry their provisions to the top, where at any rate they need not lack water. This is the story of the Round Tower at Windsor, and of other Norman towers on other mounds elsewhere. Here the ditch remained dry, for to have raised the river water to such a height would have taxed their powers, and moreover it would have leaked through the porous chalk of which the hill is composed. But the well is there. Its mouth, curiously, is beneath the carpet of one of the bedrooms in the tower, at its northernmost point, and a rope 165 feet long would be required to reach the fresh drinking water at the bottom. The construction of such a mound at the behest of the Normans is shewn in process in the famous tapestry at Bayeux; and indeed anyone interested in this period of our story could not do better than invest a florin in the King Penguin booklet about this tapestry, under the admirable editorship of Sir Eric Maclagan.

To return to the seaside. The mound finished, a quadrangle could be marked out on either flank, with the mound blocking access from one quadrangle to the other, and a rampart thrown up around both of the courtyards thus created. To make a single controlled link between them, an archway, the prototype of the Norman Gateway at Windsor, could be made through the sand on one side of the mound: and if we can imagine the beach to tilt, as the castle hill does sharply on its western side towards Clewer, then it would be natural that the only entrance from without, i.e. King Henry VIII's Gate (Plate 13), should be placed at the lowest point so that the attackers, if successful, would have to fight uphill.

At Windsor it was neither necessary nor practicable for the Normans to construct their ditch along the north side, on the brink of the escarpment; but until the eighteenth century it survived along the east side of the castle, where the flower bed is now in Plate 8; it flanked the south front, descending the slope to King Henry VIII's Gate, and ran down what is now Thames Street to the Curfew Tower. It defended also the Round Tower, on both its sides; and indeed the only point at which it can still be seen is in the moat garden, which makes beautiful the western aspect of the Conqueror's mound.

The outer trace of the castle was thus laid down by the Normans from the start, and an air photograph taken at that time would have revealed a plan identical with that of to-day. But no building-stone exists at Windsor, other than the native chalk rock, or clunch; and while this serves tolerably for wall filling it will not withstand the erosion of rain and frost as a facing material. Moreover the Normans had no quarrymen, nor masons; neither would their fresh earthworks have borne the weight of stone walls. And they were in a hurry; within two decades they ran up some 85 castles in various parts of the country, and one at York took only eight days to construct.

Although they had no stone they did not, as we have seen, lack timber; and they commanded unskilled labour in plenty. They felled the trees, lopped the branches, pointed the baulks, and rammed them home to form a continuous palisade, around the two courtyards and around the crest of their central mound. This primitive form of defence was not perfect (for does not the Bayeux tapestry show us a wooden construction being fired?), but at least their unwelcome soldiery could sleep more soundly within the compound than without; and perhaps we should not err in picturing the Lower Ward as serving not only to shelter the troops with their horselines and stores, but also to laager such cattle and swine as they might impound from the surrounding countryside.

Sometimes, as at Carcassone and elsewhere, the early castle builders provided an outer skin to their fortresses, much as if the pavement wall down Thames Street to-day was indeed an extra fortification instead of a mere fence (Plate 19). In that event we can picture the enemy, if they succeeded in breaching it, running hither and yon where the grass now is, blindly seeking an entry into the castle itself, but finding themselves penned in an *abattoir* under the flail of the defending bowmen. Although this was not the case at Windsor the design here was less naïve than, with the object of simplification, it has been made so far to appear; for there was in fact an inner line of defence, so that the enemy, on panting up the hill, would still find hot work ahead of them before reaching the foot of the mound. Upon attaining the top of the Lower Ward they would have been confronted with a deep ditch, 100 yards long, which spanned the castle from the brink of the northern escarpment across to the southern palisade. This is why the forecourt to the Deanery is sunken (Plate XI): and indeed the whole Deanery, which runs from this point back as far as the North Terrace, lies along the ditch of the Conqueror's transverse earthwork. The Lord Chamberlain's offices, running parallel but on a higher contour, tower above it; for they stand upon the elevated area known as the Middle Ward, above this ancient ditch. Thus although the accretions of time have overlaid and obscured the Norman defences at this point, these were nevertheless formidable: and let it be observed that this inner defensive apron only existed on the western side of the Round Tower, indicating that from the outset it was the Upper Quadrangle which was regarded as the inner penetralia, towards the defence of which the military architecture should be directed.

Chapter 2

THE PLANTAGENETS

IT takes time for displaced earth to harden; how long, a digression at this point may make plain. The gardens of Frogmore House, in the Home Park at Windsor, contain an artificial mound similar to that of the Round Tower. It was created from the clay excavated when the ornamental water was laid out in Queen Charlotte's 'little paradise', and we may take its date to be 1795. The temple at its summit (Plate XVI) houses the remains of the Duchess of Kent, mother to Queen Victoria and aunt to the Prince Consort; for she, not relishing the prospect of sharing a crypt with her august in-laws, with whom her relations had not always been easy, had expressed a desire to be buried in the garden of the house which had been her home during the last twenty years of her life.

Now until 1936 there was living in the Home Park a retired gardener called Mr. Barker; and he, it is pleasant to record, liked to speak of the affection in which the Duchess was held by her servants—of whom he was one, for he had been for several years a garden boy at Frogmore at the time of her death in 1861. The temple was designed at the direction of the Duchess herself, and she would lie on her sick bed in Frogmore House listening to the clink of trowel on stone as its walls rose. Mr. Barker used to say that in order to obtain a firm footing it had been necessary to sink a shaft through the heart of the mound to the gravel below; and he would add that the garden boys during their dinner hour used to scramble to the top and gaze into the depths of the pit to exchange sallies with the labourers, who chose to maintain that they were making a place for the Prince Consort to smoke in.

The Frogmore mound would then have been in existence for perhaps 70 years, and yet it was not firm enough to support the small temple. We may infer that a century would not be too much to allow before imposing the greater weight of the Round Tower upon the other mound within the castle. And this was, as near as makes no difference, the time that it was given: from about 1080 when it was thrown up, until 1180 when King Henry II, the first Plantagenet sovereign, replaced with stone the wooden stockades of his great-grandfather William the Conqueror.

Those whose nerve is stronger than their patience may be observed to decapitate their boiled egg instead of cracking and peeling the shell. This is, in effect, what the Plantagenets did with the Norman mound in order to obtain a level stance for their stone tower. But with the lapse of time the mound had settled into an uneven circle; and this, it may be hazarded, accounts for the peculiar shape of the tower that is called Round—for in fact it is little more circular than square. Its southern flank is straight, and its western and northern flanks are hardly bowed. Although this form is irregular we may picture its creators as being content; for what did they require? Since the walled refuge should accommodate as many people as possible it should extend to the edge of the platform; and moreover it was better that the ground should drop sharply from the foot of its walls. The garrison too must be able to see, by means of arrow-slits, what was happening all the way round the skirts of the Keep, without such blind spots as there would have been at the corners of a square building. But on the other hand a square house is undoubtedly more convenient to build, for nobody would be anxious to steam and bend timbers made of heart of oak. Between these conflicting considerations the present shape is, intentionally or not, a compromise. Observed in plan it is as if they had set out to design a square tower, chamfered three of the corners, and then cut a more ample slice off the fourth corner, at the north-east point, above the stairway from the base of its mound.

If a line be drawn north and south through the transepts of St. George's Chapel it may be said that the whole castle lying to the east of it was walled by King Henry II. He also threw a stout wall across the waist of the castle, along the top of the Deanery ditch; and at its northern end, where it joined his new curtain wall, he built Winchester Tower—for this had been standing for a century before the time of William of Wykeham, who reconstructed it later. In the course of his 35 years King Henry II thus constructed about half a mile of lofty masonry out of such materials as were at hand in a countryside devoid of quarries, and it is worth sparing a thought for the manner in which a piece of work so massive and so enduring was accomplished. The lead for the roofs of the many buildings which he also erected was brought from as far away as Cumberland, but the materials for the walls were close at hand: indeed the chalk rock with which they were filled was already on the site. The characteristic stone with which they were faced, then as now known as heath stone, came from the beds of Bagshot Sand which underlie that area of heath and pine about ten miles south of Windsor: the name Collingley often appears in the early account rolls, and this may be identified with Collingwood, a mile south-west of Bagshot. Here it is found embedded in the form of rounded boulders, of the type which may be seen to-day in the artificial cascade terminating Virginia Water. These blocks were split, perhaps with the aid of heat[3], into the cubes with which almost the whole exterior of the castle is faced. The church tower (*c.* 1400) of the adjacent village of Chobham is similarly built in its native heath stone.

If visitors sometimes find it difficult to credit the castle with its full antiquity, one of the causes is the nature of this heath stone, for being a silicate and crystalline material it is washed clean by every shower of rain instead of retaining the grime of the town which is swept across it by the predominant south-west wind. To those of a more reflective turn of mind the windows also may introduce an element of doubt. In the days when the curtain wall was first built the defenders would perforce have been content with mere slits, rather high up; for proper windows would have been a source of weakness, even had the glass been available, and those which pierce the outer walls to-day reflect a condition of security the very absence of which made the building of the castle necessary. Moreover in certain places the ancient curtain wall has needed refacing, and notably along the street front, after it was scraped clear of houses in Victorian days. But the essential fact remains that the outer walls and towers of the whole castle date from within half a century either side of the year 1200; and if this seems hard to realise, it is largely due to the exemplary care with which they are to-day maintained by the Ministry of Works.

During the turbulent reigns of Richard Cœur de Lion and his brother King John little was done to the castle beyond the pounding of the Round Tower with cannon balls during the abortive siege of 1216; but between 1220 and 1230 the great work of King Henry II was brought to completion by his grandson Henry III, who walled the western end of the Lower Ward. It is noticeable that the towers built by the grandfather, before the Third Crusade in 1189, are square in shape: such are the pair in the Canons' Cloister which flank the top of the Hundred Steps (Plate 7); the Winchester Tower; the four along the East Front; and the Augusta Tower and the York Tower along the southern flank. But in the half-century which elapsed before King Henry III's resumption of operations, the science of military architecture had advanced a further step, and those which he then built display the D shape, found for instance in the Krak des Chevaliers, which lies rather similarly along its craggy escarpment in the deserts behind Damascus.[4] At Windsor the type is seen in the tower miscalled King Edward III's Tower (Plate XIV); in King Henry III's own Tower, at the southern end of the cross-wall along the Deanery ditch; in the small drum tower halfway up the Lower Ward, and in its three sister towers on the western wall, along the street front (Plate 18).

Water supply provided one of the chief problems in siege warfare: no water, no resistance. It was very well to site the castle 120 feet above the river, but every drop consumed by man and beast had to be raised from somewhere; it was manifestly improvident to rely upon bringing Thames water up in barrels, since the garrison would have been cut off from the river if beleaguered. Not only must the castle be independent, but within it there must be a well so placed as to serve the troops in their last stand; it was for this reason that they added a further forty feet to their borehole so that there should be a well available at the summit of the mound on which the Keep stood. But in the desperate fighting which would follow upon hostile penetration no man could say what portion of the castle might find itself isolated, so a single well within the Round Tower would not suffice, however secure it might be; and this quite apart from its inconvenience of access and inadequacy of supply. They sank accordingly two other deep wells, one in each courtyard: one is under the grass of the Upper Quadrangle, midway between the Sovereign's Entrance and the State Entrance, and the other is in the Lower Ward, within the shadow of St. George's Chapel at its north-west point, where the pump still stands. Both date from the mid-thirteenth century; and in addition rainwater cisterns were at the same time installed on the Round Tower.

Chapter 3

KING EDWARD III

WHAT kind of lodgings were inhabited by Henry III and his precursors we can only surmise, for the earliest buildings in the Upper Quadrangle to-day were built by King Edward III. He was born in the castle in 1312, was known as Edward of Windsor, and ranks with King Charles II and King George IV as one of the most important figures whom we shall have to consider. The founding and laborious construction of the castle was now already finished, and with its completion the need for such a stronghold declined. Henceforward we shall have to deal less with the slings and arrows of primitive warfare than with the progressive adaptation of a gloomy fortress to the needs and comforts of the sovereign in an era of more established tranquillity and advancing standards of domestic comfort.

Writing two centuries later, Holinshed, in his chronicles, records of the year 1359: "In this year the king set workmen in hand to take down much old buildings belonging to the castle of Windsor, and caused divers other fair and sumptuous works to be erected and set up in and about the same castle, so that almost all the masons and carpenters that were of any account within this land were sent for and employed about the same works, the overseer whereof was William Wickham, the king's chaplain, by whose advice the king took in hand to repair that place, the rather indeed because he was born there, and therefore he took great pleasure to bestow cost in beautifying it with such buildings as may appear even unto this day."

It was in 1356 that William of Wykeham, the founder of Winchester and of New College, was given charge of the King's Works, and he held the post for five fruitful years. His tenure saw the building of the square tower known to-day as Governor's Tower, half-way up the Lower Ward, to serve in the first instance as belfry to the Chapel. To him also we owe the range of Military Knights' lodgings from that point up the hill towards King Henry III's Tower; these he built to house the Chapel Clerks, or singing men.

William of Wykeham's immediate predecessor had in the early 1350's already built for King Edward III extensive works in the region of the Canons' Cloister and the Dean's Cloister, together with a great part of the Deanery itself; it would be tedious to particularise, but the detail is set out in St. John Hope and displayed in the admirable plans thereto.

The surveyor who came after William of Wykeham built a fresh set of royal lodgings where the State Apartments now stand, and lined the whole of the eastern and southern flanks of the Quadrangle with residential buildings. What he did to the towers along the East Terrace is revealed in Plates 5 and 8. As built by King Henry II these had been elevated watch-towers spaced out along the curtain wall, their outside measurement being only about 20 feet from front to rear: the white quoins of

Hay Wrightson

HER MAJESTY QUEEN MARY

I. NORMAN GATE. Rebuilt in 1359 by King Edward III to guard the steps up to the Round Tower or Keep, and to bar access from the Middle Ward into the Upper Ward which contained the King's lodgings. Note the groove for the portcullis to slide in, and one of the three large holes in the crown of the arch.

Portland Stone half-way back along their depth show this. Now that King Edward III was adapting his castle to the purposes of a king's residence he found it convenient to add depth to these shallow turrets in order to render habitable the chambers within the thickness of their walls.

The castle, however, was not yet so outmoded as a fortress but that it was still desirable to look to its defences, and in 1362 we find King Edward III rebuilding the stone stairway leading up the mound to the Round Tower, together with the old Inner Gatehouse, known as Norman Gate, the function of which we may now consider. Let it be supposed that the enemy had carried both the Lower and Middle Wards in their onward and upward sweep towards the Round Tower and the sovereign's quarters that lay behind it. On attaining the circular ditch they could not bear to the right because Wyatville's modern road around that segment was in those days barred by the high incurving curtain wall. They must therefore follow the left-hand course, keeping the Round Tower ditch on their right, until they found themselves confronted by the Norman Gate: and here they would be brought up before the portcullis, or running gate, which slid down the groove shewn in Plate I. In the roof of the arch may be observed one of three large holes, down through which the defenders would pour whatever they had that was most disagreeable; while all the time the attackers would be raked by the fire of bowmen stationed in the crenellated gallery, known as the Apron or Chemise, at the base of the Round Tower. The essential point in the whole castle was the Keep, for to it in the last resort the king himself might be driven to repair; and the key to the Keep was the stairway which led up to it at its north-west sector. It was this vital spot that the Norman Gate, with its complex defences, was devised to screen: nor must we overlook the further fact, obscured by the later operations of Wyatville, that the stairway has still its own square fourteenth-century defensive tower at its top, which was also rebuilt at this time by King Edward III.

It has been convenient hitherto to assume that there was only a single gate to the castle, namely the one at the bottom of the Lower Ward which now bears the name of King Henry VIII. The needs of the Upper Ward were however partially served by the existence of a postern, or narrow side-entrance, with its oaken footbridge across the ditch near the south-west corner of the Quadrangle. We find it mentioned as early as 1260, and its seems from first to last to have borne no other name than the Rubbish Gate. It gave access to the gardens, which were situated on the south-tilted slope outside: no doubt the produce came in by that way, and perhaps it is not indelicate to suggest a compensating traffic through the Rubbish Gate to the gardens in return. The convenience of a direct entry to the portion of the castle inhabited by the king and his household may be presumed to have made itself more insistent when King Edward III lined the Quadrangle with residential buildings, by which time the narrow, defensible postern had perhaps come to be regarded as needlessly restrictive. At any rate we find him in 1368 replacing it with a gatehouse resembling that "Norman" Gate which he had built a few years previously: its nature can be estimated from certain fragments that remain in the basement regions between Lancaster Tower and St. George's Gateway, and a minor subsidence in the lawn outside recently revealed the vestiges of the bridge across the ditch. The bills shew that in 1537 a new double door was being ordered for the prison in this gatehouse. Both bridge and gate survived until the alterations made by Wyatville for King George IV.

Not only were there in the early days the main entrance in the Lower Ward and the subsidiary Rubbish Gate in the Upper Ward; there were further the sally ports. These were shafts driven beneath the curtain wall at certain points, and terminating in the castle ditch. Their purpose is not hard to surmise; they afforded a secondary means of entry should the gates be sealed by the besiegers, or the drawbridges which served them be demolished. Three of them survive to this day, and there may have been more originally, particularly along the northern escarpment. One of them descends from the ground floor of the Curfew Tower and, after running southwards for about 20 yards, turns as if to cross the street; but like the others it stops at the point which was formerly the bottom of the castle ditch. The next issues from the south flank of the Quadrangle between York Tower and Augusta Tower, to reach its conclusion under the grass verge to the roadway outside. Both of these can be entered, being in good condition; their walls are hewn through chalk rock and need no shoring timbers. The third goes out under the East Terrace towards its southern end, and terminates in the flowerbed; this one is now blocked by a furnace. These sally ports attract picturesque legend as a ship's bottom gathers barnacle and weed; but their true purpose was nothing more mysterious than to act as gills so that the castle could still breathe if its mouth was clapt up.

We have already considered the magnitude of the task which had been undertaken two centuries earlier in the construction of the first stone walls around the castle. The works upon which King Edward III was now engaged consisted chiefly of ranges of domestic buildings, and these called for oak beams, as well as freestone for dressing windows and chimneys and for constructing the extensive and beautiful vaulting of the undercrofts—for the hard heath stones, which had to be split, could not be worked into the shapes necessary for these purposes (Plates 36, 37). Not that the heath stone had fallen into disuse, for together with clunch it was the only building material hereabouts, and whenever walls were rising there was likely to be no unemployment at Collingley. Thus in 1365, to name only one year, no less than 156,200 heath stones were split there by Henry le Smythe—whose name may imply that he used fire in the process. As for the oak, we learn that each baulk required two carts and sixteen horses to drag it the 15 miles from Sonning to New Windsor. But the freestone must have taxed them most, for it had to come from afar. They brought 1,000 to 1,500 loads of it annually from the quarries at Merstham and Reigate; and this was taken across country for 10 miles to Kingston-on-Thames, whence it was worked up a rougher river than we know for some 35 winding miles against the stream. As much again came from Taynton, in the valley of the Windrush above Oxford, from quarries mentioned in Domesday Book; and this was dragged overland through Burford and Culham to Henley, whence it was floated down the Thames.[5]

Let it be recorded at this point that when, in 1950, the masonry of King Edward III's period was being repointed, between King John's Tower and the State Entrance, oyster shells were found embedded in the mortar, convex side upwards, as horizontal packing between the courses of heath stone: they are also found in the apron wall of the Round Tower, and doubtless at other points also, such as the stretch of late Norman walling which links Norman Gate with the Magazine Tower, or Powder Mill (Plate 6). A like practice was followed in the building of Eton College in 1441, some eighty years later: "they were only ye upper shells of oysters," we are told, "and used where ye stones did not exactly fit, to thrust in among the mortar, and to key up the work."[6] This is of more than casual interest on account of its bearing upon the medieval treatment, much in evidence at Windsor, known as galleting. Gallets (French *galets*, pebbles, shingle) are the chips of stone which fly from the mason's chisel, or the shivers of flint produced in flint-knapping, one of the oldest crafts known to man: those now being used at Windsor are in fact procured from the ancient flint-knapping district of Grimes Graves, near Brandon, in Suffolk. Since the absence of information on the subject of galleting gives rise to fanciful conjectures, it will not be amiss to spare a thought to it here.

The heath stone facing of the older walls of the castle (flanking the pavement along the north side of the Quadrangle, for instance), is composed of rugged stones of uneven size: some of them, particularly in the lower courses of the battering foot, may be as much as three feet in length and half as much in height. Let it be considered how delicate would be the job of steadying such a block upon its bed of soft mortar; and the more so since this close-textured heath stone lacks suction, as the masons say, and takes as unkindly to the mortar as would a block of glass or glazed tile. The stones were consequently chocked up with gallets, which took the weight and prevented the mortar from bleeding, to use the trade term.

The art of maintaining level beds of masonry with stones of varying size is less difficult if the mortar joints are broad, thus allowing a certain degree of flexibility in the coursing. This wide pointing is characteristic of the older portions of the castle masonry. Now mortar varies in hardness according to its constitution: at best it is less durable than heath stone, and it may be that another reason for inserting flint gallets was to ensure that they, at any rate, would resist indefinitely the scouring of rain and frost.

The structural purpose met, it is both right and natural that the treatment should serve at the same time such decorative ends as it would lend itself to. To employ galleting in brickwork, where the bricks are uniform, light and porous, would be a costly affectation; neither is it suitable in dressed ashlar, where the stones fit tightly to each other. But in districts where flint or Kentish ragstone is the native material galleting often adds distinction to the builder's craft. At Windsor, apart from its agreeable effect in adding sparkle to the texture of the masonry, it affords to the practised eye a convenient indication of date. Here and there glimpses may yet be seen of galleting in its original condition, but for the most part it was done afresh, and after a meanly imitative fashion, by Wyatville, who repointed the castle in a dismal mortar of black ash. Then followed a period of Victorian primness in which the heath stone (or may it not at that time have been sarsen stone from the grey wethers of the Marlborough downs?) was machined to a depressing exactitude, so that the stones fitted with the precision of ashlar, leaving no room for galleting: this may be seen for instance in the Curfew Tower and the Royal Mews. Finally, in 1937, the Ministry of Works embarked upon an extensive programme, replacing Wyatville's funereal pointing with a mortar of pleasing tone, into which the flint gallets are so set as to produce a flowing, cable-like effect around the stones. So far, by 1950, the interior walls of the Quadrangle have been thus repointed.

Chapter 4

ST. GEORGE'S CHAPEL

GREAT as were the achievements of King Edward III in the sphere of building, it is with the foundation of the Order of the Garter that his name is more immediately linked. It must suffice for our present purpose to say that, as originally constituted, his Order was to consist of 24 Knights in addition to himself and the Black Prince, and their spiritual welfare was to be the concern of a college of priests instituted for the purpose. By letters patent dated 6 August 1348 he laid down an establishment of 25 canons under a dean; and since it was not to be expected that the Knights themselves would be able to assemble daily for mass, the college was further to include 26 Poor Knights, who should be officers of gentle birth decayed in the wars, to attend mass and pray for the souls of the Knights of the Garter. The new Order was to be illustrious, but it was also to be Christian; and hence it would need a chapel of becoming splendour for the observance alike of its daily ritual and of its occasional solemnities. All the Orders of chivalry have their spiritual home; that of the Bath is at Westminster, of St. Michael and St. George in St. Paul's Cathedral, and of others elsewhere—normally in London, for the sake of convenience. The Garter alone, at once the oldest and the most renowned, was housed from the outset by the Lord Edward of Windsor within the walls of his patronymic castle.

Not that a chapel had been lacking before: far from it, for King Henry I had been married in the castle as early as 1121. Henry III had in 1240 built a new one where now the so-called "Albert Memorial" chapel stands; and this, in 1348, was being served by eight chaplains. To these were now added sufficient to raise the personnel of the college to its new establishment, half of them being styled canons and the remainder priest-vicars (later minor canons). The chapel itself was refitted in 1350 with a new roof and new painted windows; and it was furnished at the same time with stalls, over which hung the swords and crested helms of the new Knights, in token of their defence of the holy church.

For 135 years this small chapel served as the shrine of the Order of the Garter. That it was built at a lovely period we are reminded by the slender arcading of its northern wall, which still flanks the Dean's Cloister; and also by its fine west front, which now forms the end wall of St. George's Chapel, behind the altar (Plate 28). Of particular elegance was its entrance door, covered as it formerly was with scarlet gesso, and embellished as it still is with elaborate scroll work of wrought iron signed by the craftsman *Gilebertus* (Plate 29). King Henry III had himself endowed the chapel in 1240 with an image of Our Lady in silver gilt which weighed over a hundredweight, and there was in addition a large wooden St. George clad in armour. Upon his election in 1417 the Emperor Sigismund, brother-in-law to King Richard II, presented the heart of St. George. No man could do more. As late as King Henry

VIII's time it was customary for the gospel-reader to tender it to the Sovereign and the Knights, to be kissed by them in turn.

Poets of the first rank do not make so frequent an appearance in the story of the castle that the entry of Geoffrey Chaucer upon the scene can be overlooked, though it was for a period of less than two years. As Clerk of the Works to King Richard II he received instructions on 12 July 1390 to put in hand the repair of this chapel, which, although only forty years had elapsed since its founding, had already become unsafe. "The King to our well beloved Geoffrey Chaucer, esquire," so the commission opens, "know that we have bidden you do all such things as be needful to repair the chapel in our castle of Windsor, which is threatened with ruin and in danger of falling to the ground." The works which he carried out required a large amount of stone and caused the daily services to be removed to an adjacent building while they were in progress; but they were perhaps too little or too late, for they did not extend its life for long. A subsequent survey of its foundations and walls revealed so advanced a condition of decay that in 1478 King Edward IV resolved to replace it by another and altogether more glorious building. If this should outshine the chapel lately built just across the river at Eton by his rival and victim King Henry VI, so much the better.

The fabric so conceived, in pride of man and fear of God, is that which we honour to-day as St. George's Chapel. It was brought into being during the half-century astride the year 1500, the point which marks the close of the Middle Ages. Of the features associated with Gothic architecture in its concluding, perpendicular phase none is lacking: the flattened arch, the vertical window tracery, the treatment of bare walls with stone panelling, that obsession with the straight line which made of every circle an octagon or a hexagon—all are exemplified here. A unity in itself, it has been largely spared both the hammer of the fanatic and the improvements of the restorer.

They first built the choir, and sealed it off where the organ now is by a partition from floor to roof: not the glorious fretted ceiling which feasts our eyes to-day, but that loftier roof of oak which, unseen, does the work whilst the decorative vault takes the applause. Here for a quarter of a century daily worship was offered in a truncated choir, of disproportionate height, beneath a wooden roof—much after the fashion of Eton College chapel, which antedates it by some 40 years and is itself but the choir of an unfinished edifice. In the new choir of St. George's everything was finished; the canopied stalls were carved and in use; the sword of the Founder (Plate V) and some 90 enamelled stall-plates of the earliest Knights had been brought across the passage from the former chapel. Structurally it might have remained so roofed, for this was no mere temporary covering, designed to keep out the rain while the real ceiling was being fashioned in stone. Indeed, as far as the rafters were concerned, it was substantial to a fault. "The roof," reported Sir Christopher Wren two centuries later, "contains a vast deal of excellent timber, and it is a fault there is so much; the architect lived too near the forest, the scantlings being too great and heavy." But from the outset they were not going to be content with a wooden roof, like Eton; the springs for the stone vaulting shewed that.

While the daily office was thus being sung in the choir the walls of the nave were rising behind the partition—with a brief intermission due to passing troubles which beset the throne. The nave roof in place and duly sheeted with lead, these masons proceeded, with an audacity startling to us, to poise beneath it (at such an interval that a man can walk along its top, only stooping if he be tall), a stone vault weighing many thousands of tons and almost flat in section (Plate 30). The walls of the nave, pierced above and below with windows, appear as frail as a dragonfly's wing; the piers supporting the stone vault are so moulded as to resemble gatherings of slender rods; and the outward thrust of the vault is subtly communicated through flying buttresses, unseen from within, to little buttresses low on the flank of the exterior (Plate 27). Equilibrium was achieved by weighting the flying buttresses with stone beasts set upon pedestals; and even then they ran things fine—too fine, as time was to shew.

But these difficulties lay ahead, unsuspected. When the stone ceiling to the nave was finished in 1503 they saw that it was good, and their ambitions vaulted with it. That was the year of the foundation of King Henry VII's Chapel at Westminster, where the groined vaulting, by the same master masons, displays an unsurpassable virtuosity. They did not seek to outdo it at Windsor when, on 6 June 1506, they contracted with John Hylmer and William Vertue for the vaulting of the choir: but we may discern a hint of their admiration in the clause that the choir bosses should be "more pendant and hollower" than those in the nave—and so they accordingly are. The agreement bound the masons not only to span the choir with a stone vault but further, as an essential and concurrent part of the same operation, to construct on the outside of the chapel the pierced parapet, the flying buttresses, the square pedestals, and the King's Beasts to sit upon them. The whole of this work, namely the vaulted ceiling of the choir and the exterior counterbalancing measures, with all the stone carving involved, cost £700 in the currency of that day.

The four massive square piers under the crossing, between choir and nave, had been designed to support a lantern tower, but this project was abandoned in favour of the present stone vault over the organ screen (Plate 33). Boldly displayed in the centre are the arms of King Henry VIII, bearing the inscription ANO XPI 1528; and these are surrounded by the shields, carved in stone and painted, of the Knights of the Garter of that time, who each subscribed towards the cost of this portion of the work.

Thus was completed after half a century the great task originally entrusted by King Edward IV to Richard Beauchamp, Bishop of Salisbury, whose badge, a snail, is liberally represented both in stone and wood in those portions of the building which were finished before his death in 1481. As for the material in which they had worked, neither of the local stones was suitable, for heath stone could not be worked into the necessary forms, nor, where the factor of safety was so slight, could chalk rubble be relied upon for the interior of their walls. Once more they drew upon the freestone of

Taynton; and they used Reigate stone, too. But a new introduction to Windsor for this undertaking was Caen stone, brought across from Normandy in great quantities for use in the interior of the chapel only.

It had been a costly work. Its accomplishment had taxed not only the pool of skilled craftsmen in the country but the exchequer, too: and when the funds of King Henry VII had failed, the task had been forwarded by the bequest in 1503 of the property of Sir Reginald Bray, of whose munificence no less than 175 reminders are included among the decorations of the nave. Sometimes these take the form of his initials or his coat of arms; but more frequently to be observed is his punning badge of a hemp-bray, for bruising hemp.

Bray's benefaction, however, came late in the proceedings. Right at the start they had realised that if means could be found for attracting a stream of pilgrims the project could be nourished by their alms. Now it happened that at North Marston, a village some 30 miles north of Windsor, there was the shrine of a former rector, John Schorne, who was widely venerated on account of his ability to cure the ague and other maladies. He is still commemorated by the jingle

> Master John Schorne, gentleman born,
> Who conjured the devil into a boot,

and there are several representations of this singular feat in various churches, particularly in Norfolk and Suffolk. He had died at North Marston in 1314. Had his bones rested in the diocese of Salisbury their translation to Windsor might have been accomplished with little difficulty; for Richard Beauchamp combined in his own person the offices of Bishop of Salisbury, Dean of Windsor, and Master and Surveyor of the Chapel "and of divers other works there to be newly constructed". But North Marston was situated in the diocese of Lincoln, which in those days stretched as far south as the river Thames. It was necessary therefore to appeal to the Pope, Sixtus IV; and he, in April 1478, was so obliging as to grant a *Bulla pro Translatione Magistri Johannis Shorne*. In November 1479 a licence was granted to the priory of St. Peter's monastery, Dunstable, to exchange their living of North Marston for that of Weedon Beck in Northamptonshire, which belonged to the Dean and Canons of St. George's; and in the following February, to sweeten the pill, the King released the monks of Dunstable from their obligation to furnish certain annuities with which they had been charged "time out of mind" in consideration of their having at His Majesty's request made this exchange. We may assume that the parishioners of North Marston were not the losers by this arrangement, for we know that they set up an image of Master John Schorne, in place of his bones, and that this (as well as Schorne's well in the parish) continued to attract the pilgrims. Indeed when the Reformation came, quite shortly afterwards, they claimed to have lost no less than £500 a year by the suppression of the Schorne cult[7]—and how much that meant we are able to assess when we remember what Messrs. Hylmer and Vertue were prepared to do for £700.

We have seen that the nave of St. George's Chapel was the first portion to be vaulted

II. GEORGIAN STALL CARVINGS. This is one of the four stalls added in 1790 by Henry Emlyn, who chose for its decoration the attempted assassination of King George III by Margaret Nicholson on 2 August 1786. The four stalls in question are the pair nearest to the altar on either side.

III. ORIGINAL STALL CARVINGS. In the example here shewn a boar eats out of a cooking-pot, while the sow above suckles her young. At bottom-right is the turned-up seat of the pew, shewing a monkey birching its mate. At top-left is the stall-plate of a former Knight of the Garter.

IV. CONSECRATION MARK. Of the six consecration marks which have survived, all but this are on the outside of the building, and have consequently almost perished. The white rose of York, enrayed by the sun, was the badge of King Edward IV; and for this purpose it was ensigned with a crucifix.

V. SWORD OF KING EDWARD III. The ceremonial sword of this King, who founded the Order of the Garter in 1348, once hung over his stall in the original chapel, and is now fixed to the back of the altar in St. George's Chapel. Note the consecration-mark above, shewn in Plate IV.

VI. WROUGHT-IRON DOOR FITTINGS. These examples of John Tresilian's craftsmanship, dated about 1485, serve the door of the chantry priest who said mass for the soul of King Edward IV. Between the grille at the top and the keyplate below is a circular doorplate embodying the Garter; presumably a thong hung from the central hole, so that the latch might be raised from outside.

VII. THE CHOIR OF ANGELS IN ST. GEORGE'S CHAPEL

VIII. THE CROSS NEYT BOSS. This boss, at the south-east corner of the chapel, shews King Edward IV and Bishop Beauchamp kneeling on either side of the Cross Neyt, the chief treasure of the college in pre-Reformation days. It contained a fragment of the True Cross.

IX. THE STONING OF ST. STEPHEN. In the Hastings Chantry, upon the back of the oak choir-stalls, is a sequence of four representations of the martyrdom of St. Stephen. Painted about 1485, they are crude in technique but vibrant in feeling. In the first, St. Stephen preaches; in the second he is indicted; in the third (illustrated here on the left) he is being stoned with local flints, while Saul, at bottom-left, holds the garments of the stoners. In the final one his soul, a naked mannikin, is borne by the angels to God.

in stone. To this general statement a small qualification must here be made, for in fact the easternmost tips of both the narrow choir-aisles were given their fan tracery immediately their roofs were on; and these were therefore the first portions of the building to be completed, prototypes as it were of the greater edifice that was to be. They thus formed little chapels about 40 feet long and 12 feet across, on either side of the altar. The one on the north flank was dedicated to the commemoration of King Edward IV, whose tomb it contained. Its counterpart on the south side of the altar seems to have been designed as a focal point for pilgrimages while the great work proceeded, and it was here that the Dean and Canons hastened to enshrine the bones of John Schorne. The tower above is still known as Master John Schorne's Tower to-day: the upper chambers in it, where now the choir boys practise, originally formed the Chequer, or counting house of the college. The central boss of the aisle vault below commemorates the fragment of the True Cross, pride of the principality of Wales, which had been brought home in triumph in 1283 to King Edward I (Plate VIII). This Cross Neyt, as it was called, was now installed here also; and for good measure King Richard III constrained the monks of Chertsey to surrender the bones of the saintly Henry VI, which he caused to be reinterred at the same spot in August 1484 (Plate 31). That the pilgrims shewed their appreciation we may infer from the stout iron money box which offers 20 coin-slits for the convenience of the faithful: it has also, significantly, four locks fitted with different keys, that four officials should be present at its opening.

Space forbids the enumeration of all the treasures of artistry that the chapel contains, but something must be said of the ironwork attributed to John Tresilian, which is unmatched in this country and scarcely excelled elsewhere. The wrought-iron gates of 1483 which stand across the tomb of King Edward IV are a marvel of delicacy and skill (Plate 34).[8] Above them is the chantry chapel dedicated originally to the memory of that sovereign, with the wooden oriel later inserted by Henry VIII for the convenience of Queen Katherine of Aragon, whose pomegranate badge it bears. Her father Ferdinand of Aragon had married Isabella of Castile, thus uniting Spain into one monarchy: and this is the reason, unnoted hitherto, why the royal beasts are cavorting up the ridges of the roof to a *Castile* at the top. Across the aisle behind Tresilian's gates is a small door; it gave admittance to the spiral staircase for the use of the priest saying mass in the chantry above for the soul of King Edward IV. The hand of Tresilian is evident again in the iron fittings on the door (Plate VI). Below the judas is a beautiful handle-plate embodying the Garter; no doubt a thong for lifting the latch hung from the hole in its centre.

As the chapel had grown, so it had been consecrated piece by piece; and on each occasion the masons provided a *rose-en-soleil*, the cognisance of King Edward IV, ensigned with a crucifix. The one shewn in Plate IV is at the back of the altar, and five more examples survive on the outside of the building, marking the progress achieved up to the king's death in April 1483. The stone carvers were kept busy. All round the interior of choir, nave and transepts, at clerestory level, runs a choir of angels delicately worked in stone: at ground level too, in the side-chapels and the little chantries, their loveliness was spared by Cromwell's smashers. Occupationally clad, they were feathered to neck and wrist to meet the rigours of inter-stellar space and canonical etiquette (Plate VII).

Nor were the woodworkers idle. In the rich stalls, made by Robert Ellis and John Hilles in 1478-83, no occasion for embellishment was missed. The misericords under the seats depict scenes from the bible, the history book, the farmyard or the fancy. In front of the Prince of Wales's stall Our Lord is ascending into the clouds with only His feet protruding. The misericord of the Sovereign's seat shews the meeting of King Edward IV and King Louis XI of France on the bridge at Picquigny on 29 August 1475—a topical subject at the time of its carving. In Plate III a boar may be observed taking its dinner out of a pot while the farrow enjoy theirs above; and the under-seat at bottom-right shews a monkey birching its mate. In 1786 George III decreed that the sons of the sovereign should be Knights of the Garter, which called for the addition (in 1790) of two new stalls on either side. His architect, Henry Emlyn, did well in designing topical scenes for their spandrels, quite in the spirit of his fore-runners. In one King George III may be seen driving to St. Paul's Cathedral on St. George's Day 1789 for the thanksgiving celebrations for his recovery. In Plate II we are shown his attempted assassination by Margaret Nicholson on 2 August 1786 upon alighting at the garden entrance of St. James's Palace: we see the beefeater and Mr. Toplin, the king's footman, performing the actions which brought them £100 and £50 respectively from His Majesty afterwards.

The heraldic plates affixed to the stalls range from that of Ralph Lord Bassett (*c.* 1390) to the present day, and the earlier examples in particular form an assemblage of medieval enamelwork of the greatest rarity and technical interest. Finally a word must be said of the two early paintings on the backs of the choir stalls, the one in the Hastings Chantry dated about 1485, and its counterpart in the Oxenbridge Chantry dated 1522. Plate IX shews the right-hand half of the former, depicting the story of St. Stephen. On the left he is being stoned with local flints before the king, who wears a fool's cap; at bottom-left, as the legend beneath records, Saul holds the garments of the stoners. On the right the saint has collapsed among the flints; and two angels bear his soul to Our Lord, who is seated upon a nebuly cloud and wearing the triple tiara of the Pope. The Hastings whom this chantry commemorates was the Lord Chamberlain upon whom the anger of Richard III fell like a lightning stroke on 12 June 1483. "By St. Paul, quoth he, I will not to dinner till I see thy head off. It booted him not to ask why, but heavily took a priest at adventure and made a short shrift, for [Richard III] made so much haste to dinner. So was he brought forth and his head laid down upon a log of timber and there stricken off, and afterward interred at Windsor beside the body of King Edward."[9]

In 1681 the Dean and Canons, concerned for the safety of the chapel, invited Sir

Christopher Wren to make a survey. Repeatedly he found that the great oak tie-beams, where they had formerly borne upon the side-walls, had rotted at the ends, owing to leakage of rainwater through weak spots in the lead: or the timber roof was "much damnified by the gutters which are faulty above it". With equal sense and moderation he suggested that a quarterly inspection of the roof be undertaken, to cleanse the gutters and prevent the growth of weeds; "for drips happen suddenly, and one shilling seasonably expended prevents great charges, and sometimes incurable damages, in such fabrics as this, where the butments are too nice and tender and may easily give way to the vault, which the architect hath designed with boldness enough, low and flat to ostentation. Yet I judge he hath done what is just sufficient, if it be well maintained." To such an extent had it been neglected that many of the King's Beasts had fallen into the gutters, breaking the lead and seemingly being allowed to lie where they fell. "I could wish the Beasts might be taken off," Wren observed, "and in lieu of them pineapples added." Acorns would have been more in keeping, but pineapples were the latest novelty: King Charles II's gardener (appropriately called Rose) had just succeeded in raising them in this country, and there is a painting in the castle shewing him on bended knee presenting one to the King. We see one, too, used as a decorative motif on the undercarriage of King William III's silver table in Plate 51; and another surmounts the stone case by Cibber (*d.* 1700) in the East Terrace garden.

The beasts were accordingly removed, but no pineapples replaced them. Just two centuries later, in 1884, Sir George Gilbert Scott was called upon to give attention to the vault of the nave, which was again shewing disturbing signs of spreading outwards. It is pleasant to record that such new stone gargoyles as he found it necessary to supply were carved in the medieval tradition, recording contemporary events. Disraeli is there, and Mr. Gladstone with his legendary axe; and a soldier may be seen administering a pill to a crocodile, in jocular allusion to the departure of British troops to fight Arabi Pasha in Egypt.[10]

More extensive by far were the works undertaken between 1921 and 1930 under the direction of Sir Harold Brakspear, when the roof and vault of both choir and nave were taken off, mended, cleaned, and strengthened in the re-assembling. In the course of this remarkable feat underpinning was carried out at various points, particularly at the south-west corner of the nave, where the foundations were found to be insecure; bold buttresses were built for the first time around the outside of the transepts; and an array of new King's Beasts, designed by Joseph Armitage, were placed upon the pinnacles after an interval of two and a half centuries.[11]

Chapter 5

THE LOWER WARD

OF the three divisions into which the castle falls, the Upper Ward and the Middle Ward are appropriated to the use of the King. The Lower Ward is the domain of the college of St. George, with its chapel in the centre and its buildings grouped around. Upon the east side lies the Deanery, on the north the canons' houses, on the west the music (the organist and singers, with the belfry and library), and on the south the Military Knights—to use the name by which the Poor Knights have been known since 1833. Although its buildings are wholly contained within the castle, the college from earliest days has claimed and enjoyed the freehold of the pearl within the oyster. Let us now consider the various elements which compose its establishment.

The old chapel, condemned as unsafe and beyond repair, had been abandoned in 1483 when the daily services had been transferred to the choir of the new St. George's. Ten years later King Henry VII resolved to raise upon its site a tomb-house for the burial of King Henry VI as well as himself. Avaricious at all times, he had inherited the burden of the unfinished St. George's Chapel, the building of which continued throughout his reign into that of his son. No doubt therefore it was a relief when Pope Alexander VI, in October 1494, suppressed two English monasteries and devoted the proceeds to this new mausoleum. The old chapel of 1240 was accordingly pulled down, and the one that took its place is the one now known as the "Albert Memorial" (Plate 26). It was slightly smaller than its predecessor; in fact the new one would just have fitted inside the old. It was roofed with wood and lead, according to the procedure which we have observed before; but the serried buttresses indicate that a stone ceiling was intended, and the springers for the vault inside confirm it.

At this point a dispute arose which held matters up, as it proved for ever. The monks of Westminster claimed that the Abbey was the recognised royal burial place, and that King Henry VI had not only been their parishioner but had actually, so some averred, chosen the place of his sepulture among them. Upon this the monks of Chertsey claimed that they had been wrongfully dispossessed of their prize. The college of St. George, possessing the bones, coyly rebutted both claimants. The matter was referred to the chancellor, who pronounced in favour of Westminster. Thereupon the King, in July 1498, declared his intention of building the chapel for himself and King Henry VI at Westminster instead of Windsor: but in order to secure so lucrative an accession the Abbey authorities would not object to contributing the sum of £500, which would represent about half Vertue's bill for the stone vault to their new chapel. The Pope, for his part, was content that the money from the two suppressed monasteries should be switched to the Westminster Chapel, and his successor inaugurated its commencement in 1503 by suppressing two more. The monks of Westminster had finished paying their £500 by Christmas 1500; but when the King died in 1509 the bones of King Henry VI were still at Windsor—and there they have remained.

Between 1511 and 1514 the great Thomas Wolsey occupied a canonry at Windsor, but since he was at the same time Dean of Lincoln, York and Hereford, the tranquillity of the cloisters was perhaps not unduly disturbed. When he was cardinal, some ten years later, he secured this chapel as his own tomb-house, and the finest Italian craftsmen of the day were set to creating for him a monument of so sumptuous a nature that it is tempting to digress into a description. The singularity of its fate is well known. When Wolsey fell, in 1529, King Henry VIII seized the tomb and had it re-tailored to his own measure. But after a time he abandoned the idea, and a few weeks before his death decided to be buried with his "true and loving wife Queen Jane" in St. George's Chapel, midway between his stall and the high altar. The unfinished monument lay in the disused chapel until in 1646 the Roundheads sold its metalwork. The four great candlesticks found their way to the church of St. Bavon in Ghent; the pair in the sanctuary of St. George's Chapel (of which one shews in Plate 34) are modern replicas of them. In the deserted chapel only the empty sarcophagus and its base remained; being of marble they were unsaleable.

Ashmole had it from Dr. Stokes, a canon at the time, that it had been the intention of King Charles I to turn the chapel into a royal mausoleum. King Charles II had an unfulfilled plan, devised by Wren in 1678, for replacing it by a rotunda, like the Radcliffe camera, to house the remains of the Martyr King: he contented himself, however, with having the interior painted by Verrio, and whatever further intentions he may have had were cut short by his death in 1685. Once more the abandoned chapel fell into neglect, and when Joseph Pote wrote his history of the castle in 1749 its ornamentation was "hastening to decay". In 1810 King George III, who had realised as early as 1794 that there was only room for one more coffin in the royal burial place in Westminster Abbey[12], took up the floor of this chapel and hollowed out beneath it a vault to hold forty-eight coffins. This involved the removal of the tomb of Wolsey and King Henry VIII, of which the strange destiny was now to be fulfilled—for to-day it houses the remains of Lord Nelson in the crypt of St. Paul's.

King George III evolved a new idea for the use of this problem chapel, namely to convert it into a chapter house for the Order of the Garter; and for this unfulfilled qurpose 300 wooden shields of past Knights were painted, of which a number may be seen in Plate 36. For King William IV, Wyatville added the present stone-vaulted roof, on the lines evidently intended when it was first built in 1494. Finally, after the death of the Prince Consort in 1861, Queen Victoria revived the conception of forming it into a mausoleum, and to this end its walls were lined by Sir George Gilbert Scott with alien marble. Equally incongruous was the name with which this Tudor chapel was thereupon invested—for the true Albert Memorial is at Frogmore. But criticism falters in the presence of sorrow so total and so desolating; and the interior of the Albert Memorial, this alabaster box, very precious, impels respect and may even come to command admiration.

In the eighteenth century it was customary to speak of St. George's Chapel as the cathedral; and this was natural, for not only had it a dean and canons, but there were cloisters as well. The cloisters were an appendage to the "Albert Memorial" chapel, or rather its precursor upon the same site; for they were built by King Edward III for the college (consisting of two quadrangles) which was to serve his new Order of the Garter. Its bachelor priests in those pre-Reformation days were housed in college rooms on staircases, as at Oxford and Cambridge; these were disposed round the inner cloister, with the twelve canons upstairs and the twelve priest-vicars on the ground floor. The dean, as head of the college, was accommodated in the adjoining cloister, which served the whole community both as covered way to their devotions and for airing and recreation in rough weather. When going to mass they would use the porch shewn in Plate 22, which led through the present vestry of the canons to the west front of the old chapel (Plate 28). This they would enter by the ornate door, to cross the ante-chapel (now the entrance into the cloisters), and so proceed to their stalls in what is to-day the "Albert Memorial". A new priest would soon feel at home, for the domestic arrangements of the college followed a pattern familiar in the Middle Ages. There would have been a common dining-hall, with screens, buttery and kitchen; indeed we know that William of Wykeham built them in 1357, but since with the change in social habits they have disappeared it is idle to speculate upon their former whereabouts.

The Canons' Cloister was built for the new college in 1353 upon the site of certain former royal lodgings. Although with the introduction of wives and other civilising adjuncts it has lost something of its monastic character, it remains one of the most picturesque corners in the castle. The timber-framed houses overhang, rather crookedly, a penthouse passage all the way round, and across it runs a covered way from the Dean's Cloister to the top of the Hundred Steps. These led down the escarpment to the canons' graveyard, which is presumably the chapter garden to-day. The houses along the north side of the cloister (i.e. the left flank of Plate 24) rest upon the curtain wall of the castle, which is older by some 175 years; from the white-washed interior it is not easy to realise that embodied in these residences are original square towers of 1180, like those along the east front of the castle.

The Garter priests who served the earlier chapel were thus cramped into a back courtyard from which their outlet was along the passage to the larger cloister, and thence through the pretty porch out into the microcosm of the Lower Ward. Their living quarters were inexpensively run up out of local timber, brick and plaster. Their outer cloister was constructed at the same time but on a scale at once more ample and more costly, for the tracery around its central garth called for Reigate stone. This has needed replacement from time to time, but on the whole the Dean's Cloister compares not unfavourably with contemporary examples elsewhere (Plate 23). Its wide ambulatory is flanked on either side with stone seating, and it is pleasant to note that this is drilled here and there for the ancient game of "nine holes".[13] Over the north-west corner is a small medieval strong-room, known as the Aerary: the ecclesiastical records, stored here in a large press of the fourteenth century, reach back beyond the foundation of the Order of the Garter into the late 1100's, when the curtain walls to the castle were being built.

The inconvenience of these close quarters in the Canons' Cloister soon made itself felt, for as early as 1409 we find the college being granted by King Henry IV the area immediately north of St. George's chapel, on the ground that they were "not fully endowed as to houses and lodgings for their vicars, clerks, choristers and servants". To these new precincts it was the priest-vicars who migrated, into a set of chambers built for the purpose, of which only their stone hall remains; and this since 1693 has housed the Chapter Library.[14]

But this arrangement in turn proved of short duration; for when Bishop Beauchamp started building St. George's Chapel for King Edward IV he at the same time (1478–81) erected the Horseshoe Cloister at its west end in order to house the priest-vicars (Plate 25). The arms of the horseshoe originally extended a little further eastwards, so as to clasp the end of the chapel; and since the cloister contained 21 houses it presumably housed not only the thirteen 'petty canons' but also the eight priests who, until the Reformation in 1550, served the various chantries within the chapel. A drawing by Paul Sandby in the time of King George III shews the Horseshoe Cloister bisected from north to south by a brick wall, with a stonemason's yard on the chapel side and a garden on the other. Its houses in those days were plastered. They had fallen into disrepair by 1870, when £9,000 was spent upon their restoration under the care of Sir George Gilbert Scott. Although a certain newness in their appearance is still a little disturbing, the work was done faithfully, for we know from the original accounts that they were timber-framed houses with brick filling and embattled cresting. This change of key into brick for the domestic buildings of the college warms the heart and is instantly agreeable after the sunless grey stone of the castle precincts. Nowadays, when the establishment has dwindled to three canons and three minor canons it is good and joyful to add that they dwell together in the inner cloister once more, and the Horseshoe Cloister is the abode of the Lay Clerks (or men singers) and Vergers.

To disclose that continuous thread of human activity which is the very marrow of history, let it be here recorded that, while the present account was being written, one of these gentlemen, scratching the soil in the Horseshoe Cloister to plant a garden, exposed a silver coin of the reign of King Edward IV and a brass counter about the size of a shilling. The latter, known technically as a jetton, was minted at Tournai in the third quarter of the fifteenth century; and thus it might even be one of the fourpennyworth of counters which we know were bought in 1460—or the further half-pound of them added for sevenpence in the following year. The counting-house for

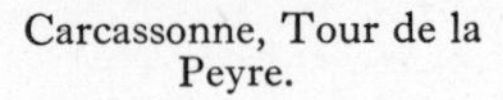

Carcassonne, Tour de la Peyre.

The Curfew Tower, as Wyatville intended to make it.

the college was, as we have seen, the upper room in Master John Schorne's Tower; here the treasurer would sit, in his exchequer, at a table spread with a chequered counting-cloth, scratching his head over the calculations brought upon him by Bishop Beauchamp's operations in St. George's Chapel and the Horseshoe Cloister.

The Curfew Tower, at the north-west salient of the castle, dates from 1227 and has fine vaults underneath (Plate 21). It has formed the belfry of the college since Bishop Beauchamp began building St. George's Chapel in 1478; before that the ring of eight bells hung in the square tower half-way up the Lower Ward, now the residence of the Governor of the Military Knights. Each bell had its own personality and name: Mary and Jesus were the two biggest, and then came George, Edward, John, Aston, Wyron, and the "cope bell". Plate 20 shews the original oak staging which now supports the bells in their massive cage above. Strange it is that a structure so impressive should emit so gentle a sound. The present clock, made by John Davis of Windsor in 1689, still plays every three hours the same little tune ("St. David's") in a senile and stringhalt fashion; it then breaks into peals of merriment, laughing with all its bells—and thereupon goes through the whole performance twice again.

Wyatville, concerned like other restorers with the royal apartments, never reached the towers along the western wall of the castle, which nevertheless were in a bad way; the middle one in particular was abandoned and in ruins, having no roof, back or floors. Edward Blore restored the southernmost one (Salisbury Tower) in 1840, and Anthony Salvin did the other two in 1860 and 1863. The Curfew Tower, having been in continuous use, was in tolerable shape, but all three had to be refaced after the removal during that period of a range of dwellings which had attached themselves to the curtain wall on the street side. Occasion was taken by Salvin at the same time to invest the Curfew Tower with its present top (Plate 19), obviously copied from that which Viollet-le-Duc had placed upon the Tour de la Peyre at Carcassonne. So notable in fact is the parallel that an extract, in translation, from the Report of the Historical Monuments Commission of France (1855–79, Volume 3) is worth recording:

> Since 1855 the work of restoring and consolidating has been in progress. In 1852 the Emperor, passing through Carcassonne, was greatly struck by its impressive aspect, and eager to retrieve these forsaken ruins. Every year a sum is assigned for restoring the most damaged or interesting portions, and several have already been roofed after their original fashion. Lastly, each year sees the acquisition of some of the hovels which have grown up against the walls, and already the isolation is largely accomplished.

X. THE NORTH TERRACE LOOKING EASTWARDS. In the foreground is the eastern end of Queen Elizabeth's Gallery, leading to the turreted oriel of King Henry VII's building—where Queen Anne received the news of Blenheim in August 1704. On the left James Wyatt's frivolous turret claws the corner of the Star Building erected by Hugh May in 1678 for King Charles II. Wyatville has disfigured its bands of Portland Stone (below the string courses) with imitation jointing.

XI. THE FORECOURT OF THE DEANERY. This sunken area is all that remains of the Norman ditch which until 1678 separated the Lower Ward from the Middle Ward. The gothic sash windows on the ground floor light the former Chapter House of 1350.

It was in 1855 that the Emperor Napoleon III paid his first visit to Queen Victoria and the Prince Consort and stayed for a week in Windsor Castle: it would be remarkable had he not alluded in the course of his visit to the work which he was then initiating at Carcassonne.

If it be thought, as it universally is, that the fashions of Carcassonne are less becoming in Windsor, there is a certain negative solace in the reflection that what Wyatville was intending to have done to the Curfew Tower, had he got round to it, was even less pleasing. War and fire are, after all, only the chief out of many hazards to which old buildings are exposed. We may be glad that a like fate did not befall the other towers along that conspicuous and beautiful front (Plate 18).

Where had the Poor Knights been living during the first two centuries of their existence? It is not a question that need trouble us much, for the reason that few appointments to the office had been made—perhaps because no lodgings were provided, or no endowments set aside for their pensions. Be this as it may, we know that there were commonly only one, occasionally two, and rarely as many as three of them at any given time. In his last will, however, King Henry VIII had re-established their foundation, reducing their nominal strength from 26 to 13, but making provision for their payment: and in 1557 Queen Mary Tudor took steps to furnish them with seemly accommodation—the same lodgings in fact which they inhabit, to the same number, at this day. The former Belfry Tower, half-way up the Lower Ward, she converted into a residence for their Governor; her arms together with those of King Philip of Spain may be seen in stone over its entrance. The range of buildings above this tower, which King Edward III had built in 1359 for the singing-men of the former chapel, she caused to be adapted, almost indeed rebuilt, for the provision of lodgings for six Poor Knights. For the remaining seven she built lodgings along the curtain wall below the Belfry Tower, linking it with King Henry VIII's Gate (Plate 12). The stone was floated down the Thames from Reading Abbey, which her father had suppressed eighteen years earlier. The bills make callous reading: they shew payments to the labourers for digging Caen stone out of the windows of the Abbey for battlements in the new lodgings for the Poor Knights, and to the masons 'for taking downe the greate stones of the dores and windowes in the Chapell of Our Lady there.' No wonder Reading Abbey to-day looks like a last year's bird's nest.

Chapter 6

KING CHARLES II

ANYONE who traces the story of the castle will be struck by the frequency with which both its outer walls and the buildings which they enclose are said to be in a ruinous condition; indeed the wonder is not that some portions are new but that any are old. To read, in Hope's book, the survey made for Queen Elizabeth, when the conies in the ditch undermined the foundations and the 'choughs and pigeons' nested in the crannied walls, or the later reports made successively for James I and Charles I, is to view with a new understanding the works of reparation entailed upon their posterity. While it had been a fortress its walls had been kept in repair; but then the residential buildings were simpler and made smaller demands upon the royal purse. As the castle became a palace its upkeep outstripped the capacity of its owner and we find the sovereign increasingly confining his attention to his own quarters in the Upper Ward. In the outworks decay was neglected to the point of peril, so that it was cheaper to demolish than to recondition. Thus, for example, in 1671 King Charles II pulled down the great towered gate-house, with its drawbridge over the ditch, which in former days had separated the Lower from the Middle Ward (Plate 3). In Queen Victoria's time not one house only but several ancient and picturesque buildings were cleared away in the precincts behind St. George's Chapel and at the foot of the Lower Ward: and the "Albert Memorial," that Tudor chapel for which successive sovereigns had been at a loss to suggest a use, might well have gone the same way had not the cloister behind been linked with its survival.

Apart from repair and maintenance, habitations many centuries old call for periodical remodelling. In 1549 the boy King Edward VI had complained of the castle, "Methinks I am in a prison; here be no galleries, nor no gardens to walk in";[15] and it requires but a slight acquaintance with the personality of King Charles II to realise that he would not content himself with a house last rebuilt at the time of Poitiers. It is true that a certain amount had been done to it in the intervening centuries. King Henry VII had added for his queen the tower with the turreted oriels which now forms part of the library (Plate X). His granddaughter, Queen Elizabeth, had extended this, as if remedying the complaint of her puny brother, by a gallery for exercise in inclement weather (Plate 52); and outside it she had rebuilt in stone the North Terrace which her father had first contrived in wood. For her it formed a convenient way from her apartments to the Little Park 'where her Highness must needs make her walk'; for King Henry VIII, who walked less, they had provided upon it a target 'for the King to shotte at with his handgonne.'

But these were only Tudor tinkerings with a Plantagenet residence, and King Charles II, who had acquired modish habits during his exile in France and Holland, found the house little to his taste. Across the Channel the palace of Versailles was disclosing its quarter-mile frontage to the gaze of the world; in its courtyard stood an equestrian statue of Louis XIV, whose triumphs Lebrun was displaying upon the ceilings within. In the Louvre (the summer is 1665, the observer Wren) "no less than a thousand hands are employed, some in laying mighty foundations, some in raising vast stones by great and useful engines; others in carving, inlaying of marbles, plastering, painting, gilding, &c.; which altogether make a school of architecture, the best probably at this day in Europe. An academy of painters, sculptors, architects and the chief artificers of the Louvre meet every first and last Saturday of the month. Bernini's design of the Louvre I would have given my skin for, but the old reserved Italian gave me but a few minutes view."[16] Vast indeed were the works in progress over there, but it is with the spirit rather than the scale that we are concerned. "Painters, sculptors, architects and artificers"; that was the team, and that the order, noted by the rising young architect. It was not lost upon him that while this modernistic style of the Baroque, sweeping up from Italy, was the joint work of various craftsmen, it was the painter among them who took precedence. St. George's Chapel, too, had been the harmonious product of a team, and its craftsmen had presently transferred their group of skills to King Henry VII's Chapel at Westminster; but their intention had not been pictorial. There the main virtuosity had been that of the architect, to whom the sculptor, and still more the colourist, had been subordinate. In the new order of things it seemed that the builder and the carver were there to provide a suitable setting for the display of the painter's powers.

It is however a popular fallacy to link Wren himself with the castle. Admittedly it had been familiar to him from boyhood, for between the ages of 3 and 27 it had been his home, his father being Dean of Windsor until 1659. It was Wren's drawing of the castle from the north that Hollar had etched in 1667. In 1678 he produced for King Charles II the plans for a circular tombhouse for King Charles I which were not adopted. It was to him that the Dean and Canons turned for advice when St. George's Chapel was tumbling down in 1681—and not unnaturally since, apart from his family connection, he had rebuilt St. Paul's Cathedral and half the churches of London. But it was not until 1684 that he became Comptroller of the Works at Windsor—and King Charles II, whose building operations were by that time completed, died twelve months later. For King William III, Wren later evolved some grandiose and incongruous plans for the Italianisation of the Upper Ward; and not the Upper Ward alone, for he would have destroyed the Horseshoe Cloister to provide a vista of the west end of St. George's Chapel, and would have made of the Round Tower an *ara coeli* by means of a wide classical stairway from the foot of the mound. But this, like his proposed mausoleum, was merely a castle in the air. The prosaic truth is that the only building executed by Wren within the castle was a new guard-room for the soldiers, at the outset of King James II's reign in November 1685; and of this, which ran southwards from Winchester Tower, no trace remains.

So if not Wren, who was King Charles II's architect at Windsor? Hugh May, the friend alike of Pepys and of Evelyn. And although he is by a long way the lesser figure, to Hugh May is due the credit of introducing the grand Baroque conception into the domestic architecture of this country; for the building at Windsor upon which he and Verrio and Grinling Gibbons collaborated foreshadowed the finest examples elsewhere. From it stems the association of Wren with Verrio at Whitehall and at Hampton Court, as well as Wren's partnership with Thornhill in St. Paul's Cathedral and Greenwich.[17] The carvings of Grinling Gibbons may be seen in all but the last-named.

Let us then consider what Charles II and Hugh May did; and first in that section of the Upper Ward which comprised the royal suite and is known to-day as the State Apartments. Here, in September 1675, they demolished a section 170 feet wide of King Edward III's range of building, and replaced it by a rectilinear block instead of the former varied and irregular plan. Seen from the outside the new building was of unrelieved dullness, four storeys high, with a plain parapet diversified neither with turrets nor battlements; a mere box, of which the windows were round-topped (and on the ground floor *œil-de-bœuf*). The only ornamentation was a big Garter Star upon its northern face, and hence came its name—the Star Building.[18]

But the plainest box may hold the richest contents, and nothing was spared within. On its south side, along the flank of the Quadrangle, they surprisingly retained the Gothic undercroft of 1362 (Plate 37), and upon this were superimposed the two saloons shewn in Plates 38 and 39. Queen Catherine of Braganza, whose rooms these were, is seen in highest heaven among the gods, or beatified as St. Agnes over the mantelpiece (Plate 40). In the dining-room Grinling Gibbons allowed his fancy full rein, providing a profusion of game, fish and fruit, carved in limewood with matchless skill and exuberance. *C'est magnifique, mais ce n'est pas la guerre*. Lebrun at Versailles had the martial achievements of Louis Quatorze to immortalise: Verrio at Windsor could only veil the recreations of Charles II behind the threadbare conventions of classical mythology. Nothing could be further removed from the context of a castle: in person one is at Windsor, but in spirit one is gaping with Pepys at the voluptuous splendours of Whitehall.

All the State Apartments partook of this nature in King Charles II's day, although only three of them have retained the paintings which lent them their distinctive character. Most striking were the domestic chapel and St. George's Hall, which together made up the long chamber shewn in Plate 55. The eastern (or further) portion was St. George's Hall: the nearer portion (just less than half) was the chapel, and both are preserved for our admiration in the illustrations to Pyne's *Royal Residences*. The loss of these Caroline interiors is calamitous, for they were important documents of taste and beautiful in themselves, despite their not unwelcome incongruity. Their destruction is laid at the door of Wyatville, and certainly they were out of keeping with the taste of the Gothic Revival. Though he declared that he would have spared the ceiling of St. George's Hall had its condition warranted it, Wyatville lost no sleep over its removal. "Architects, painters, sculptors, and many persons of taste do not greatly value this ceiling", he observed. Those however who assume that he lacked cause for his action would do well to consider, in Ambrose Poynter's account, the state of delapidation in which he found it.

In his diary of 16 June 1683 John Evelyn wrote, after visiting the castle, "Verrio's invention is admirable; his figures move; and if the walls hold (which is the only doubt, by reason of the salts, which in time, and in this moist climate, prejudice) the work will preserve his name to ages." It was not so much the efflorescence of salts which proved their undoing, but the perishing of the keys by which the ceilings are suspended. When plaster is squeezed up between the laths it over-bulges; and it is the overhangs, or keys, which are in fact responsible that the whole ceiling, weighing several tons in the case of one of these saloons, does not crash to the floor. But the keys are brittle, and they snap if there be percussion or shaking on the floor above, apart from the intrusion of damp or other domestic mischance. The rooms shewn in Plates 38 and 40 have each, during the past twenty years, been filled with scaffolding while their ceilings, by now as tender as eggshell, have received skilled treatment at the hands of the Ministry of Works: and the former had already been restored in 1798.[19] If two out of three would thus have fallen within two decades, how many of the original twenty would we expect to have survived for 250 years?

> We will grieve not, rather find
> Strength in what remains behind.

The rebuilding of the royal apartments was one of the achievements of King Charles II, and another was his continuation of the North Terrace around the outside of the Upper Ward on its east and south flanks. But his most spectacular contribution was the Long Walk. For his uncle at Versailles André le Nôtre had conceived the perspective of the Grand Canal (1668), which began at the far end of the *Tapis Vert* and conducted the eye seemingly to infinity. At Windsor there should be an avenue three miles long, leading far out into the Great Park: and if it should end in the middle of nowhere, where did the Grand Canal end? Where does William III's great avenue at Hampton Court end? The vista was a purpose in itself: let it only be long enough and the manner of its conclusion became irrelevant.

The Long Walk must have looked in early days much as it does in Plate XIII; but it came to an abrupt conclusion at the foot of the final rise to the castle. Here it would have to cross the main road to London (Park Street to-day); and when it reached the castle walls it would be necessary to pierce an archway into the Quadrangle. But the first thing was to lay out the *longue allée* and plant the four rows of young elms; while they were growing the King's design could reveal itself. What he would have done we shall never know, for the planting had only begun when, in February 1685, he died. He is commemorated by his equestrian statue, which stands finely at the foot of the Round Tower, its gaze fixed upon that portion of the building which we owe to his taste (Plate 14).

Chapter 7

KING GEORGE III

IF King Charles II had done his best to mould the castle to his taste it was through no admiration for its Gothic quality, but rather the reverse. He was the product of his age, and his was the age which Inigo Jones and Sir Christopher Wren had taught to admire the classical models. Consistently throughout the seventeenth century the slow beat of the pendulum had swung the mind of patrons from the Gothic towards the Italianate style: indeed in St. George's Chapel we have already caught the first whisperings of these airs from the Mediterranean. In the upper half of Plate 34 there are two oriels; they were originally identical, both of stone, in the prim style of 1485. But King Henry VIII demolished the right-hand oriel to replace it by the present *bombé* one in wood; and since it bears the cognisance of his Spanish consort we may assign to it such a year as 1515. There was no purpose that the old oriel could not have served equally well; it was a foretaste of the art of the morrow, the first swallow of a summer that was to mark the eclipse of the Gothic style.

With the death of King Charles II we enter upon the Dark Ages as far as Windsor is concerned, for a further century was to elapse before the pendulum swung back. If Wren had executed his visionary plans for King William III they would have been in the high classical tradition; but instead he built Kensington Palace and largely rebuilt Hampton Court, leaving the castle alone. Queen Anne was devoted to Windsor for the sake of the stag-hunting; during the reign of her uncle King Charles II she and her husband had formed the habit of residing in a house opposite the south flank of the castle, and when she became Queen she moved across into the State Apartments but did not make any changes. To say that the first two Georges never visited Windsor would be untrue, but only by a narrow margin, for they disliked the place and grudged the money to keep it in repair.

When King George III came to the throne as a young man of 22 he was already steeped in the classical taste. "The King and Lord Bute," wrote Horace Walpole to a friend in January 1761, "have certainly both of them great propensity to the arts. Building, I am told, is the King's favourite study."[20] This would naturally interest Walpole, who for the past seven years had been indulging a puckish fancy at his new Gothic villa at Twickenham. Across the river, almost within sight from the windows of Strawberry Hill, Sir William Chambers had been giving lessons to George III in the schoolroom at Kew, taking Italian architecture for his theme and illustrating it by the erection in the royal gardens of a series of classical temples. These (when they were not Chinese) were faultlessly Roman, for as yet only the most advanced intellectuals were flirting with the Gothic heresy: clever young men like Horace Walpole—and his friend Gray at Stoke Poges, with his moping owls and his ivy-mantled towers.

Things had not been easy for King George III in childhood. His parents had been on bad terms with King George II, and when he succeeded his grandfather on the throne he never wanted to see the scene of their quarrels at Kensington and Hampton Court again. In fact he never did. He conducted his official business at St. James's Palace in London, where he further acquired Buckingham House for his bride, Queen Charlotte; and for the rest he continued to use his mother's little house at Kew as a retirement in the country.

As for Windsor, it would have been as strange for the Court to go into residence there as if Their Majesties were to resume the use of the palace of Hampton Court to-day. The castle had not been used since King George III was born; not in fact for close on half a century, and vested interests had sprung up. Information about the castle during the Dark Ages is hard to come by, but it seems to have been gradually parcelled out into "grace and favour" residences. Thus in 1773 a Mrs. Kennedy took up residence in King Henry III's Tower,[21] and there is reason to think that she succeeded a Mrs. Craster (née Catherine Villiers).[22] Mrs. Margaret Trevor had enjoyed apartments within the castle for some years before her death in 1769.[23] Mrs. Egerton, in June 1767, entered into occupation of the tower at the north-east corner of the Quadrangle;[24] and in the following year Mrs. Walsingham[25] (daughter of Sir Charles Hanbury-Williams) established herself in a suite of rooms on the south side, eastwards from King Edward III's Tower. These people were private residents; unlike the Surveyor-General of the Office of Works, who appropriated the present Garter Room as his drawing office.[26]

Mrs. Walsingham had to move out in August 1783, because her apartments were assigned to the Prince of Wales upon his coming of age and being granted a separate establishment. She had been apprehensive as early as 1776[27]; and no doubt this was due to the intelligence that the King himself was looking for a *pied-à-terre* at Windsor. He had offered his brother the Duke of Cumberland £6,000 a year to give up the Rangership of Windsor Great Park, with Cumberland Lodge which went with it, but the Duke had declined.[28] In June 1776, the month of Mrs. Walsingham's insecurity, he resolved to take over the little house which Queen Anne used to inhabit before her accession. The Lord Steward had recently relinquished it, and while the King was making up his mind who should have it next, "the Queen," as he wrote to Lord North, "expressed a strong wish that, as Queen Anne had lived there, I would give it to her; this will give us the means of some pleasant jaunts to that beautiful Park."[29] In the following year (October 1777) the Queen paid the Duke of St. Albans £4,000 for the house which he had inherited from his ancestress Nell Gwyn: it forms the married quarters of the Royal Mews to-day.[30] This habitation, only 200 yards down the slope, became known as the Lower Lodge, to distinguish it from Queen Anne's old house, which was henceforth known occasionally as the Upper Lodge, but more usually as Queen's Lodge.

Since their union had been blessed with a generous number of children, Sir William Chambers extended Queen's Lodge eastwards, producing a barrack-like building, lying parallel to the south flank of the Upper Ward and only 40 yards away from it. Two storeys high, it stretched from opposite St. George's Gate to-day, across the line of the Long Walk to a point opposite Augusta Tower, shutting out the view of the park from the rooms in the castle. Between the two royal buildings ran the public footpath from Windsor to Datchet, which came up Castle Hill from the town and descended through the Home Park to the old Datchet bridge. Queen's Lodge was sufficiently advanced by the summer of 1778 to house the parents and eight of the children, and in addition rooms were fitted up in the castle across the way for the four eldest princes with their governors and gentlemen. Miss Hamilton, who was in waiting, already made no doubt that Their Majesties would in future make Windsor their chief summer residence.[31] Queen Charlotte was enchanted. "Our own habitation is just the thing for us," she wrote to her midshipman son the next summer (1779), "and the Duke of St. Albans' house will be finished by the beginning of autumn. That being done our journeys will be more frequent and attended with less inconvenience."[32]

One deplorable occurrence coincided with the building of Queen's Lodge, namely the filling-in of the medieval ditch around the castle.[33] According to the writer Charles Knight, who lived opposite the castle entrance and was a loyal son of Windsor, it was done under architect's orders in the 1770's because "it was considered it would render the foundations of the castle more secure, as in many places they were giving way. The chalk was taken in immense quantities from a deep chalk pit sunk inside the park." Hope, on the other hand, says that the ditch served as a convenient tip for the builders' refuse during the construction of Queen's Lodge. Probably both are correct. Evidence is not lacking that it was an insanitary and malodorous adjunct to the royal residence, certainly in Wren's day[34] and doubtless before and after as well; but this was remediable, and in any event was not the cause of its unfortunate levelling.

Among the townsfolk of Windsor the good king moved with the freedom of a small squire in a country village. Upon coming to live informally among them he had not chosen to curtail the freedom with which the schoolchildren had regarded the old castle as their playground. Charles Knight, born in 1791, recorded in after-life: "The deserted courts of the Upper Quadrangle often re-echoed on the moonlit winter evenings with our whoo-whoop. The rooks and a few antique dowagers, who had each their domiciles in some lone turret of that spacious square, were the only personages who were disturbed by our revelry. In the magnificent playground of the Terrace, away we went along the narrow wall, and even the awful height of the north side could not abate the rash courage of *follow my leader*. Up from the North Terrace, and past the Round Tower garden, one came to a pile of ugly buildings, the guardhouse and its canteen, the Royal Standard. Adjoining the Deanery was a ruinous building called Wolsey's tombhouse, neglected since the days of James II. The park was a glory for cricket and kite-flying. The King would stand alone to see the boys at cricket. He was a quiet, good-humoured gentleman in a long blue coat; and many a time had he bidden us good morning when we were hunting for mushrooms in the early dew and he was returning from his dairy to his eight o'clock breakfast. Everyone knew that most respectable and amiable of country squires, and His Majesty knew everyone. There was no carriage road from the castle or the Queen's Lodge except through the town; the King and his family were forever in the public eye. There was a lawn behind the Lodge, but there was no other place in which strangers or neighbours might not gaze upon them or jostle them."[35]

Years afterwards the King told a friend that he had started with the idea of a hunting-box, for himself and the Queen to sleep in occasionally whenever he might come to Windsor to hunt, or make a family excursion and find it too late conveniently to return to Kew or London in the evening: but that he had been led on, as is common enough, from little to more, until in the end he had laid out £70,000 upon it. And he added that if he could have foreseen that Windsor would have been their chosen residence he would have prepared the castle and resided in it.[36] In fact in the summer of 1789 he clearly meant to make the move, for the private residents were told to be ready to receive the King's commands.[37] But it fell through: in October Lady Harcourt, then in waiting, reported to her husband, "I am sorry to tell you that the plan of living at the castle is quite given up. It is unfortunate; the King would not only have a habitation that would be proper for him, but the preparing it would furnish him with amusement, which he but too much wants."[38]

Lady Harcourt need not have been apprehensive, for the King found plenty of occupation. Being interested in the Order of the Garter he busied himself in St. George's Chapel, confining his attention to the choir in which its ceremonial was conducted; and presently, seeing that His Majesty had spent £16,000 upon that, the Dean and Canons felt themselves called upon to refurbish the nave, upon which they spent £6,000.[39] We need not go into the details of these operations beyond noting that no unsuitable improvements were effected—with one exception. The original stone tracery of the great East Window over the altar was demolished in order that a heroic representation of the Resurrection, after Benjamin West, might be inserted. The experiment was a costly failure apart from the design itself, as to which Horace Walpole characteristically observed that Our Lord appeared to be scrambling to heaven in a fright, as if in dread of being again buried alive.[40] It only survived for 70 years, when it was replaced by the present indifferent window in memory of the Prince Consort. It was the mercy of providence that the great West Window at the other end of the Chapel was reprieved,[41] for it contains to-day all the good fifteenth-century glass that we have. West had executed a still bigger design for that, covering 1,000 square feet of glass; this time it was to have been the Crucifixion "containing near 70 figures, many of them colossal in size".

His works in the Chapel completed, the idea of trying to bring the castle itself back into royal occupation began to work once more in the King's mind, but he made no move during the lifetime of his old instructor, Sir William Chambers. As early as June 1793, however, he promised the reversion to the Surveyorship to James Wyatt, to whom he confided that he would have fitted up the castle and lived in it had not Chambers told him that it could not be made comfortably habitable, and advised him to build Queen's Lodge instead.[42] When therefore in 1796 Chambers died the way was clear for the achievement of his design.

Catherine of Braganza, very unlike Queen Charlotte, had borne no children, and consequently a house that had suited the requirements of King Charles II was no use for King George III. He could have pulled it down, as Charles II had pulled down its predecessor, but that would have been costly; and moreover the site of the Star Building would hardly have accommodated a family of thirteen. He therefore thought out the problem afresh. Queen Charlotte should have the tower at the south-east corner of the Upper Ward; it had never been put to such a use before, but that was no reason why it should not serve the purpose now. Two of the princesses should have adjoining rooms along the east front, and the rest of the family should be disposed along the south flank. As for himself, after 40 years of happy married life, he would arrange a bachelor suite of four rooms and a kitchen on the other side of the castle. A man of the simplest tastes (he used to light his own fire at six in the morning and would never have a carpet), his choice fell upon a low and sunless apartment on the ground floor, under the State Apartments, facing north and looking out over Eton.

Money being scarce, he could not indulge in the extravaganzas of Charles II before him or George IV after, and indeed his sobriety of judgment would in any case have restrained him. But he set a few masons quietly to work replacing Hugh May's windows with well-designed Gothic ones; and his taste led him, like Wren, to use Portland stone—that finest of English materials, which possibly had come under his notice during his first visit to Weymouth in 1789. This Portland fenestration marks the difference between James Wyatt's work for him and Wyatville's work for his successor; for Wyatville's inferior freestone, though bleached where it is exposed to sunlight, retains its peculiarly unpleasing yellow tone in the shade. No doubt it was used for economy, for it is soft and can be cut with the saw; the harder Portland was costly to work.

It is the characteristic of a castle that it was designed to keep strangers out: it was only in later centuries that wealthy magnates took to focusing attention upon a Grand Staircase, as if to make the maximum impression at the outset upon their less opulent visitors. But now that King George III intended to use the State Apartments for Garter ceremonial, concerts, banquets, and balls, he needed a suitable approach. Perhaps the two staircases of King Charles II were too small, or wrongly placed, or insufficiently Gothic. Probably their Verrio-painted walls and ceilings had decayed. Be the reason what it may, James Wyatt in 1804 built for him a straight-ahead stairway at the bottom of a shaft 100 feet deep, topped with a skylight. It was not a happy arrangement. On arrival at the State Entrance the company passed beneath a dark and low vault under the Queen's Guard Chamber, to ascend the staircase in a subaqueous light—for the lofty walls were blank, with no side-openings. At the top they advanced into the Rubens Room (or King's Drawing Room as it was then called).

"I am a little of an architect," King George III once observed to Benjamin West;[43] but a fatality dogged his works. There had been the fiasco of Queen's Lodge. He spent £100,000 upon a Gothic folly at Kew, resembling the Bastille: Queen Charlotte had tried to dissuade him, but it was not until 1806, when his eyes had failed, that he abandoned the project unfinished.[44] His staircase at Windsor was similarly doomed. To begin with, it violated tradition. In any palace it was always customary for strangers to be received by the Yeomen of the Guard in the Guard Chamber; to pass thence into the Presence Chamber, where the Pages of the Presence were; and finally into the Audience Chamber. After the interview the sovereign would withdraw into his "Drawing" Room, and so return to his private apartments. But at Windsor the new staircase led the guests straight into the king's Drawing Room—which would not have mattered, to be sure, if there were compensating advantages. On the contrary, however, that room was smaller then than now; if the guests turned left along the north front they were jammed in a series of still smaller rooms; if they turned right they passed through two dull apartments into his Guard Chamber (the Grand Reception Room to-day) and thence downstairs and out through an interior courtyard.

Wyatville is reckoned a less distinguished architect than his uncle: but he had more practical sense. He barred the way into the Rubens Room, and he deflected the flow of visitors into the spacious Queen's suite overlooking the Quadrangle (Plates 38, 39), thus observing the traditional sequence. And the abolition of King Charles II's chapel, though regrettable, made possible for the first time a free circulation around the whole series of State Apartments. For it was the chapel that dislocated George III's plans and drove him to adopt a singular expedient for by-passing it. There lay along its north flank a small interior courtyard known as Horn Court: to-day it forms the Waterloo Chamber, but then it was open to the sky. This little court he now proceeded to line, along its four sides, with a two-tier cloister, flagged and open on the ground floor, but enclosed and carpeted above. It was entered at each corner by doors which still remain to give access to the present Waterloo Chamber: and thus it formed a link between the various rooms around Horn Court, and in particular it made possible the by-passing of the chapel. This ingenious solution he may well have copied from the Cloisters at his beloved Eton College; and it can hardly be doubted that it provided the basic idea for the Grand Corridor which Wyatville built twenty years later around the Quadrangle.

With the completion of his staircase and cloister King George III's essay in architecture was completed, except for the replacement of Verrio's broken ceilings in some of the rooms. Mrs. Egerton and Mrs. Kennedy, the only two of Charles Knight's antique dowagers to remain, had removed to houses found for them in the town.[45]

On the evening of Friday, 2 November 1804, the castle, empty since Queen Anne's death, received its sovereign once more. Penetrated at last by that romantic revival which swept from Walpole at Strawberry Hill to Sir Walter Scott at Abbotsford, King George III had contrived a fit background for those romantic Orders of Chivalry upon which his mind was continually harping. To Benjamin West "he said he should have thought it impossible thirty years ago that he should ever encourage Gothic architecture."[46] Probably Queen Charlotte wished he never had. After four November days in their new abode she wrote to Lady Harcourt: "We are now returned to our new habitation in the castle. Not to shock you or Lord Harcourt with my opinion on this subject I will briefly tell you that I have changed from a very comfortable and warm habitation to the coldest house, rooms and passages that ever existed."[47]

XII. ST. GEORGE'S GATE. Pierced by Wyatville at the south-west corner of the Quadrangle. The octagonal Devil's Tower was also built by him, but its square base is ancient.

XIII. THE LONG WALK. This avenue, three miles long, was first laid out and planted in elm by King Charles II in 1685. Owing to the ravages of elm disease the trees were felled in 1945 and replaced by alternate horse-chestnut and plane, with the intention later of eliminating the less successful species.

Chapter 8

KING GEORGE IV

FOR the last ten years of his life King George III was insane, and gloom descended upon the castle. He continued to inhabit his depressing rooms on the north front, and the hushed family remained on the south side. Queen Charlotte died first; he followed in 1820, and the Prince Regent ascended that throne which he had in effect occupied during the decade which had seen the downfall of Napoleon.

It had been a problem for him where to live during those years. In London he still had Carlton House for himself, and St. James's Palace for offices and functions. Buckingham House was not his; it was the appanage of his mother. His only country house was the Pavilion at Brighton, that eccentric habitation which he had built in his salad days. To fulfil the duties of the Regency he needed a house within reach of London—but the castle was out of the question. So, after examining various alternatives, he had in 1812 taken over the dairy farm appended to Cumberland Lodge in Windsor Great Park, and Nash had converted it for him into a rambling, thatched *cottage orné*, according to the mode then prevailing. It goes without saying that he too had been led on from little to more; but with the story of the Royal Lodge as it was (and is) called, we are not here concerned. The question was, where should he live now that, at 57, he found himself king?

His father, as every schoolboy knows, had been nursed on the dictum, "George, when you *are* king, *be* king." As he looked in the glass the new sovereign said to himself, "George, when you're *not* king, claim your privacy"; and if we would appreciate his position we must view it against the background of the past. His predecessors had not counted upon enjoying much life of their own. Public business had been transacted while the king was dressing—at his Levee, in fact. When Pepys's friends came up from the country, if they did not wish to see the lions in the Tower he would take them to watch King Charles II eating his dinner: and this not because he was a friend of Will Chiffinch the Page, but because it was the privilege of every loyal subject. If the butcher-boy had walked into George III's room with a tray of kidneys the king would have directed his criticism to the kidneys rather than to the boy. *Autres temps, autres mœurs*. King George IV looked at things differently.

The old king being dead, the restrictions which had been observed out of a natural respect for his melancholy condition ceased to operate. Once more in the Home Park the boys flew their kites and the good townsfolk took their walks abroad. Not on Sundays only, but every day except Tuesdays and Saturdays, the band played on the crowded East Terrace[48]—and not in the sunk garden, which did not then exist, but under the very windows of the apartments which were called private. It therefore caused a painful impression when, on 4 August 1823, King George IV closed the Terrace (except on Sundays) and the Home Park. But the local journal took it in good part: "However the inhabitants of Windsor may at first feel this measure as a privation they at the same time cheerfully acknowledge that the Castle is entirely wanting in privacy; and they hail the circumstance as the assurance that the King is about to make this glorious palace of his ancestors once more the seat of royalty, diffusing the natural advantages of his high station among the favoured residents in Windsor and its vicinity".[49]

The inference was correct. For nearly four years after his accession George IV had continued to live in seclusion in the Royal Lodge, using Carlton House when public affairs required his presence in London, and visiting Brighton when he needed a change. Now, for the first time, he was at length to gratify public expectation and take up his residence in the castle. On October 1 he made his state entry, and he remained for an experimental period of two months. The natural assumption was that he would inhabit King Charles II's rooms on the north front, as every other king had done. True, his father had indulged an old man's whim and lived on the ground floor of it, but filial piety did not demand that he should do likewise. In the event he did something quite different: he chose to live in the brighter and sunnier apartments associated with his mother and what he called the Sisterhood, on the other side. Having established the doctrine of the king's privacy, this is where he would practise it; and as for King Charles II's rooms, they could henceforward be known as the State Apartments and be used for official purposes.

Simultaneously with the closing of the terrace and the park he had ordered the demolition of Queen's Lodge, after its brief existence of 45 years. The building materials were sold on September 15 and in the following February, 1824, the local paper was able to announce that its removal had "produced the greatest imaginable improvement, throwing open the beautiful scenery of Windsor Great Park and an uninterrupted view of the Long Walk."[50] For King Charles II's avenue had grown up during the past 240 years; all that it lacked now was a *raison d'être*. The king had already built a road from its further end over the shoulder of Snow Hill to the Royal Lodge, and this he was in the habit of using when, wearing Windsor uniform and a straw hat,[51] he drove himself to the castle in a low pony chaise. Now he commissioned Richard Westmacott to execute an equestrian statue of King George III to close the vista at the far end. At the near end he pulled down three or four houses in Park Street which obstructed its passage; and, now that he had removed Queen's Lodge at the top, the way was clear at last to lead the Long Walk up through his garden to the foot of the castle wall.

But his two months' residence in the autumn had disclosed the need for works more extensive by far if the castle were to be brought to that state of comfort which the dignity of the Crown demanded; and when the Chancellor of the Exchequer in his budget speech in April alluded to the prestige of the country in the counsels of Europe at that moment in history, Parliament voted £150,000 to enable Windsor Castle adequately to fulfil its high purpose. Whether they would have done so could it have been foreseen that the ultimate cost would amount to over a million pounds (of which a quarter was for furnishing) is open to doubt. Eight Commissioners were appointed to supervise the work, and after a competition they selected as architect James Wyatt's nephew, Jeffry Wyatt, then a man of 58. He immediately took up his residence in Winchester Tower, where he remained for the rest of his life. On June 22 the king, who had been spending a second period of four months in the castle, moved out as 500 workmen set to upon the Upper Ward; and for four and a half years he directed the renovations of the castle from the tranquillity of the Royal Lodge. Thence on August 12, 1824, his 62nd birthday, he drove over to lay the foundation stone of the new archway which was to admit the Long Walk into the Quadrangle and to bear his name. It was on this occasion that, at the architect's request, the king authorised him to change his name to Wyatville, by way of differentiating himself from other members of a family distinguished in the profession both before and since. "Mr. Wyatville himself was worth seeing," an observer wrote; "a busy-bustling, vain little man, but not at all pompous, though such a man as one might expect to be gratified by the addition of *Ville* to his name."[52] "Veal or mutton," the king is traditionally said to have observed, "call yourself what you like." A daily paper, with equal point and wit, marked the occasion with a happy verse:

Portrait of Sir Jeffry Wyatville, by Sir Thomas Lawrence.

> Let George, whose restlessness leaves nothing quiet,
> Change if He must the good old name of Wyatt;
> But let us hope that their united skill
> Will not make Windsor Castle *Wyatt Ville.*

Great were the changes wrought during the next four years. It will be well to take a survey of them before entering upon the contentious subject of their merit. Plate XV shews the Upper Ward from William the Conqueror's mound, and almost every façade that is visible is Wyatville's work. He built the two lower storeys, along the south flank (in the shade) and along the east flank (to the left); they encroach upon the Quadrangle and are built against the wall of the chambers with which Edward III lined the Upper Ward in 1367. On the ground floor are offices; the first floor houses the Grand Corridor, of which the interior is shewn in Plate 56. Wyatville's also is the polygonal building in the corner; it provides the Sovereign's Entrance below, and the Oak Dining Room above (Plate 57). Behind it appears the corbelled and embattled top, containing a thousand tons of stone, with which Wyatville capped the corner tower rebuilt by King Charles II. The upper range of windows all round light the new storey of servants' bedrooms which Wyatville added. Towards the right is King George IV's Gate, which admits the Long Walk; it is flanked by the machicolated York and Lancaster Towers—and this group is by Wyatville too. In the foreground is the statue of King Charles II, for which Wyatville designed the present base; he also moved the statue from the centre of the Quadrangle because, now that he had pierced King George IV's Gate, it obstructed his new view down the Long Walk from the State Entrance. He blocked the medieval Rubbish Gate (formerly at the extreme right of this photograph), replacing it by the new St. George's Gate, which is just out of the picture on the right (Plate XII). He filled in the Conqueror's ditch at the base of the mound, which used to extend as far out as the shadow on the left, and was deep enough to contain a covered court for real tennis: had he not done this the carriages could not have reached his new St. George's Gate, as will be seen from Plate 14. Finally he removed 13,000 cubic yards of top soil from the Quadrangle, thus lowering its surface by from three to six feet; this was probably to enable carriages to enter from the Long Walk, for it is even now a steep pull through the archway for horses. It was the soil so removed, no doubt, which filled up the moat, and very likely provided also the raised walk around his new East Terrace Garden. The only feature in this illustration which Wyatville left unchanged is the small tower to the left (Clarence Tower), built by King Henry III in 1171.

Wyatville built the State Entrance, thus enlarging the Queen's Guard Chamber above (Plate 17). He built the lofty octagonal Brunswick Tower on the North Terrace, at its eastern end; and also the smaller octagonal Devil's Tower (Plate XII). He raised the Round Tower by 33 feet. He formed the East Terrace sunk garden. He completed the replacement of Charles II's windows by Gothic ones, for King George III had not got far with that task. And finally, though he did not live to see the Royal Mews completed in 1842, they were built to his designs.

Some of these measures were necessary, and were indeed the pretext upon which Parliament had granted the money. The completion of the Long Walk, for example, was overdue; and that in turn involved the piercing of King George IV's Gate. York Tower, which flanks it on the east side, was an old one, resembling Augusta Tower next to it; we must regret its transformation, but the twin towers which now flank this entrance, though unlovable, are not without appropriateness (Plate XIV). The creation of this entrance made redundant the Rubbish Gate of 1368, which was only 25 yards further west; we cannot judge the loss involved in its destruction. But we can measure the price of Wyatville's St. George's Gate, an equally small distance further on, for it involved the obliteration of William the Conqueror's moat at the foot of the Round Tower. This was a grievous loss, and one is tempted to ask whether King George IV's Gate might not have served both purposes. But it is fair to recognise that the levelling of the moat, though deplorable on balance, made possible the construction of the Moat Path (behind King Charles II's statue; Plate 14); and this, besides being a convenience, enabled the public for the first time to see the Upper Ward—for the moat, with its boundary wall, had reached almost as far as the wicket-gate in the railings which now bound the Quadrangle at this point, leaving only a narrow passage or gangway between its boundary wall and King John's Tower.

Because Wyatville's achievement was in some ways so great one feels the more his lack of refinement and, in so far as architecture can reveal it, his lack of humour too. Even without a bulldozer he did a good deal of damage, and some of his windows (notably along the North Terrace at its eastern end) reveal him as a heavy-handed designer—unlike his uncle, from whom, according to his biographer and assistant, "he learned those requisites which distinguished the abodes of Prince and Nobles."[53] And the highly medieval machicolation, which would do credit to Hollywood: it was Wyatville's introduction, for there was no example of it at Windsor before. Together with this stands or falls his grand design of raising the Round Tower, for if he had not distributed these pretentious head-dresses all round we might still have had the squat Keep that was not only in harmony with its period and purpose, but more pleasing in itself than the present edifice. Moreover its added height is a sham, for it is merely a collar of stone; from its top one looks down upon the roof of the real Round Tower where it originally was, 33 feet below. Wyatville was always thinking what Windsor would look like in a wig. He need not have worried. A group of buildings so venerable and so beloved would have looked very well without these meretricious adornments.

He was a good builder; it is curious that he should have countenanced such naïve deceits. Passing over the bogus portcullis-groove in his St. George's Gate, let us consider in detail one instance of his method. At the foot of the steps up to the Round Tower is a high wall, facing the Quadrangle. It is built in ashlar, that is to say dressed freestone, close-fitting and worked to a smooth finish. Wyatville ruled its surface with lines of a deadly uniformity, as if it were built of blocks of identical size; his masons outlined the sham blocks with chiselled grooves, which they filled with black mortar—and then, crowning fatuity, they embedded flint gallets in the purposeless mortar. No attempt was made (or indeed could be made) to conceal the real joints, which can be seen pursuing their logical course independently of this artless, disfiguring and costly imposture. The same effect could have been produced with adhesive tape.

Furthermore, he was needlessly destructive in his treatment of buildings which, after centuries of honoured existence, had established a prescriptive right to survival. There was, for instance, a certain point at the waist of the castle, on the south side of the Round Tower, where the curtain wall curved sharply in, to intersect the very mound itself; and instantly, with equal sharpness, it issued afresh, and curved round to the Devil's Tower. The wall was lofty at this point—though to be sure King George III had halved its height in 1778 in order to bring the squat Round Tower into view from the windows of Queen's Lodge.[54] To the orderly mind of Wyatville this re-entrant angle in the wall, following the trace of William the Conqueror's earthwork, was anathema. The logical course would be to girdle the Round Tower with a circular roadway: and no sooner said than done. But he could have pierced an arch through the ancient wall in question, at the south-east point of his new "Saxon" Tower, and let the traffic out that way: that is what he had already done outside his own house, Winchester Tower, to give admittance to the North Terrace. It would have saved the traffic an awkward corner upon completing his pedantic circuit; and, more important, it would have spared an exceptionally interesting portion of the original fortifications.

We are upon surer ground in commending his Grand Corridor, which would have saved King George III from crossing the windy Quadrangle to visit his family—for there was formerly no communication between the north flank and the east. Nor was there any adequate passage linking the rooms on the principal floor, whereas each suite now opens into the Corridor, which in itself forms a spacious picture gallery 550 feet in length—"My eye, what a spot for a walky walky," as Creevey wrote to Miss Ord upon first seeing it.[55] The Sovereign's Entrance at its angle solved a problem, for when King George IV decided to live in those apartments the only entrance was a plain door in the corner of the Quadrangle, so placed that his carriage could not drive up to it. Secure from criticism, too, is the sequence of drawing rooms which Wyatville contrived by re-arranging the party-walls in the east front (Plates 60–63). No doubt they owe much of their resplendent decoration to the taste of King George IV, who brought to them a quantity of material from Carlton House, including the fine doors. When required to incorporate some painted glass from the same source, "Wyatville hummed and hawed at first a good deal," as George IV wrote to his secretary, Knighton, "however I brought him at last to say that he thought 'he cud pleace soom of't to adwantage, though 'e 'ad not joust thin fix'd where'."[56] It is, as a matter of fact, the poor armorial glass in the windows of the Equerries' Staircase.

An eighteenth-century rhymester once wrote:

Who pays the piper?
"I," said John Bull:
"Whoever plays the fool
I pay the piper."

The process, not unknown to ourselves, was familiar also to King George IV, who had been Prince of Wales at the time of Trafalgar and Regent when Waterloo was won. With that distinction of vision which was one of his engaging attributes, he commissioned Sir Thomas Lawrence (upon the suggestion originally of Lady Anne Barnard)[57] to paint a heroic series of portraits of the sovereigns, statesmen and captains who had contributed to the downfall of Napoleon. Now there used to be in the centre of the north side of the castle two interior courtyards, one on either side of James Wyatt's Grand Staircase; the larger one was called Horn Court, as we have already seen, and the smaller one Brick Court. In order to provide a fitting gallery for this historic sequence of paintings Wyatville put a floor across Horn Court, and a ceiling successfully designed to illuminate the windowless chamber thus created (Plate 43). It was in accord with the character and tradition of Windsor Castle, which has always reflected a just pride in the martial glories of our past.

But this raised again the question of the Grand Staircase, for it was no use having so proud a display if access to it was by devious passages from the Rubens Room. Wyatville, at his best in contriving solutions to interior problems, now demolished his uncle's Grand Staircase, put a floor across its well (thus forming the Grand Vestibule to-day), and pierced an arch through each flanking wall—into the Waterloo Chamber on the one side and into Brick Court on the other. A reference to Plate 54 will shew the use to which he now put Brick Court. The visitors ascended some new stairs (under the carpet in the foreground), to be greeted by Chantry's statue of George IV on the landing: they then branched right and left, to come up to where the horsemen now stand. From here they advanced, behind the camera, across the new Grand Vestibule and into the Waterloo Chamber. The plan was not without inspiration: the King welcomed his guests and directed them into the gallery in which his triumphs were displayed—for unlike King Charles II he had at least some triumphs to record. The drawback was that the light at the foot of the staircase, meagre at best under James Wyatt's skylight, was now non-existent, being cut out by the new floor to the Grand Vestibule; and it was dismal for state visitors to grope their way from their carriages into a black vault. There is a picture of Queen Victoria welcoming the Emperor Napoleon III in these cavernous regions in 1855, by glimmering lamplight even in the daytime.[58] Salvin, therefore, in 1866, so changed it as to bring the guests up to the landing from George IV's right and left, and thence up the centre, as shewn in the illustration. No one has thought of a better idea since.

In assessing Wyatville's work allowance must be made for the structural condition of the building which he was commissioned to make habitable. He built Brunswick Tower because its predecessor was split from top to bottom: the Devil's Tower likewise crumbled at the touch. Since 1765 the ceiling of St. George's Hall had been menacing ruin.[59] The roof timbers in many places had rotted. Dislike the Curfew Tower as we may, the way to protect a building against the climate of this island is to provide a sloping roof with overhanging eaves, that the rain may be discharged clear of the walls. They knew this in 1180, and we must suppose that they had some reason for not using local Berkshire tiles from the first, instead of bringing costly lead from Cumberland. Presumably they needed to move about on the tops of their buildings, to confound their assailants below; and for this purpose a sloping roof would not serve. Nevertheless the fact remains that a flat roof of lead in England is an abiding liability. Expanding and shrinking with changes of temperature, the lead presently loses its resilience and needs attention and renewal. Windsor Castle covers over thirteen acres, and perhaps three or four of these have roofs from which the water cannot run off freely on account of the battlements. Wide channels run along the top of the chalk walls behind the parapet, and a choked or leaking gutter will quickly and secretly ruin the masonry underneath, as Wren had pointed out. Doctrine so simple would need no stress did it not account for many of the desperate remedies to which Wyatville was driven by his discoveries as the work proceeded.

Once such reconstruction becomes necessary, by reason of prolonged neglect such as the castle had undergone in the Dark Ages, repairs will naturally be effected in accordance with the spirit of the time. The Gothic revival was an essentially romantic movement, of which James Wyatt's admired designs for Fonthill and Ashridge were the dramatic expression. Sir Walter Scott, when staying with King George IV at the Royal Lodge in 1826, thought "Mr. Wyatville appears to possess a great deal of feeling and taste for Gothic architecture"; and this was clearly the opinion of the eight Commissioners picked by Parliament to guide the work. They included men of artistic discernment like Sir Charles Long and Alexander Baring, as well as sensible men of affairs like the Duke of Wellington. These named the architect of their choice, and he gave them the buildings they admired: it is the whole generation that is answerable for the result—and for all we are entitled to say they may have been right. At any rate they had the advantage of seeing the problems on the spot instead of trying to visualise them 130 years afterwards. Merely to glance at the insipid drabness of King Charles II's Windsor is to condone the steps which Wyatville took to restore its earlier diversity of outline; and this, after all, was one of the injunctions specifically laid upon him by Parliament.

In justice it should be remembered also that despite the large sums voted he was continually hamstrung for money. This may account both for his abandonment of Portland stone and also for the profusion of shields which have never yet received their carved armorial bearings. On 29 April 1828, for instance, King George IV wrote to Knighton: "You will hardly credit what I say when I tell you that since your departure and the perfect conviction with and in which you left me that orders would be instantly issued for the proceeding with our works, up to yesterday no one single step has been taken to carry this into effect, and that Wyatville in consequence was brought to a standstill, and was on the point of dismissing the greater part of that immense body of workmen. However I am in some hopes that [he] will not be brought to this disgraceful and really abominable dilemma, for I stated the matter *strongly* to the Duke yesterday and he *positively promised me* that he would *immediately* give Wyatville *written orders* to *proceed with all speed*."[60] Nevertheless four days later Wellington was protesting to Knighton: "I assure you that we have not a shilling. Every farthing of money that can be scraped together has been applied to H.M.'s purposes."[61]

Beset as he was with many difficulties, Wyatville achieved a great work, despite his natural limitations and the taste of the generation which his style reflects. When we admire Windsor from a distance it is Wyatville's Windsor that we see. He found a workhouse and he left a palace. He found "the coldest house, rooms and passages that ever existed"; he left a warm, dry, comfortable, well-appointed house. He did his job so well, in fact, that nothing has needed to be done to it since.

XIV. KING GEORGE IV's GATE. The foundation-stone of this new entrance, admitting the Long Walk to the Quadrangle, was laid by King George IV on 12 August, 1824. Lancaster Tower, on the left of the arch, was new; York Tower, hidden by the tree, was an old tower but raised and assimilated. Further to the left is the rounded front of "King Edward III Tower", built by King Henry III in 1223. Between it and the Lancaster Tower was formerly the medieval "Rubbish Gate" which Wyatville destroyed.

XV. THE QUADRANGLE, seen from the base of William the Conqueror's mound.

XVI. MAUSOLEUM OF THE DUCHESS OF KENT, in the gardens of Frogmore House.

In leading the Long Walk up to the castle King George IV had abolished his garden and laid it out in lawn. Where, now, was he going to find shelter from the wind and seclusion from prying eyes when he wanted to take the sun and air? All that was open to him was to pace the quarter-deck below his windows, or step down from it on to the bowling green which (like the stone terrace itself) owed its creation to King Charles II.[62] Because he had selected the East Front for his habitation, Wyatville had accorded it special emphasis and dignity by means of elaborate square-headed oriel windows (Plate 8): the plate glass which filled them, incidentally, was accounted a marvel,[63] and an enterprising thief created a stir by making off with a piece. Beneath this front King George IV now bade the architect make him a private enclosure, a *hortus clusus*, which he would deck with orange trees; and there should be an orangery, too, under the new bastion on the north side of it, with tall windows facing south to afford shelter and warmth to the trees in winter. It would look as if it were a sunk garden, though in fact it would be the same level as the ground outside; all that Wyatville would have to do would be to enclose the requisite area of ground within a high wall, and pile up against its interior stone refuse from his building operations, and perhaps some of the 13,000 cubic yards of top-soil from the Quadrangle.

"The King of France has recently presented to our sovereign 34 fine orange trees, destined to ornament the royal garden at Windsor," it was announced in September 1828; and a fortnight later the crowds on Westminster Bridge saw a floating forest as the barge laden with them passed up the river to Kew en route for Windsor.[64] From her residence in Frogmore House Princess Augusta wrote with sisterly candour: "Along the Bowling Green for about the space of three acres there is to be an old-fashioned garden with espaliers. I presume the leaves will be cartridges and the fruit made of shot; otherwise there will be nothing at all military in the appearance or intention of such a queer place."[65]

Military or not, the garden is overlooked from the house, as the King presently realised. "His mind," tattled Creevey to Miss Ord, "is quite made up never to live in the castle, which considering the hundreds of thousands which have been expended upon it is not amiss. He says it is too public."[66] He was not always easy to please. "He complained that the rooms were too small and the furniture too large."[67] Nevertheless it was in the bedroom overlooking his orange garden that death claimed him in 1830.

NOTES

[1] Hist. MSS. Comm. 7th Report, p. 479a.

[2] March 22, 1682: "The Court return next week; and after a short stay here go to New Windsor for 3 months." Hist. MSS. Comm. 7th Report, p. 351a.

[3] See article on Sarcens, by H. C. Brentnall, F.S.A., in *Wiltshire Archæological Magazine*, Vol. LI (1946), p. 422.

[4] See Crusader Castles, by Robin Fedden, 1950.

[5] There is an informative and documented article on William of Wykeham's builders and the Cotswold quarries, by E. M. Jope, F.S.A., in the *Berkshire Archæological Journal*, Vol. LI (1949), pp. 53–64.

[6] Tighe and Davis: *Annals of Windsor*, Vol. I, p. 337.

[7] Ashmole's *Order of the Garter* (1672), p. 172.

[8] Hope, for once, is in error in asserting that they were not formerly gilt; they clearly were.

[9] Thomas More's narrative, printed in Holinshed's Chronicles, ed. 1808, Vol. III, p. 381.

[10] Article [by Canon Deane] in *The Times*, 6 March 1928, p. 19.

[11] Brakspear recorded his fine achievement in the *Journal of the Royal Institute of British Architects* (Third series, Vol. XXXIX, 1932).

[12] *Farington's Diary*, June 8, 1794.

[13] A form of marbles or bagatelle: *vide* Strutt's *Sports and Pastimes* (1801), p. 204.

[14] Thus Hope: but the quarters to which the priest-vicars migrated may equally have been the adjacent house now known as No. 23 The Cloisters.

[15] J. G. Nichols: *Literary Remains of King Edward VI* (1857), Vol. 1, p. 131.

[16] *Wren Society*, Vol. XIII, p. 40.

[17] Geoffrey Webb, *Baroque Art*; Proceedings of the British Academy, Vol. XXXIII (1947).

[18] Its heath stone came from Frimley. State Papers Domestic 1675–76, pp. 300, 542.

[19] Hope, p. 348.

[20] *Horace Walpole Correspondence*, Walpole to Zouch, dated 31 January, 1761: Yale edn. Vol. XVI (now in the press).

[21] Her MS. diary is in the Royal Library. On March 8, 1805, she wrote: "I left the Store Tower after a residence of 32 years." Henry III's Tower was called Store Tower then.

[22] Private information from Sir Edmund Craster.

[23] *Horace Walpole's Correspondence*, Yale edn., Vol. X, *passim*.

[24] *Journal of Lady Mary Coke*, Vol. III, p. 33.

[25] *Mary Hamilton, ed.* Anson (1925), pp. 138, 140.

[26] Charles Knight: *A Volume of Varieties* (1844), p. 74.

[27] *Autobiography and Correspondence of Mary Granville, Mrs. Delany*, Vol. V, p. 234.

[28] *Farington's Diary*, November 22, 1793.

[29] Royal Archives; Georgian Papers, 2434.

[30] Ibid., 2631.

[31] *Mary Hamilton, ed.* Anson, p. 66.

[32] Royal Archives: photostat of Barton family papers.

[33] *Gent. Mag.*, June 1805, p. 529.

[34] "There is a small piece of void ground in the Castle Ditch at Windsor, formerly a garden, but at present a Common Nuisance, abused by the laying of Carrion and making Dunghills and emptying Jakes's upon it, which makes it very noisome to Their Majesties' Court and all persons passing yt way."—*Wren Society*, Vol. XVIII, p. 91.

[35] Charles Knight, *op. cit.*, pp. 69 *et seq.* See also his *Passages of a Working Life* (1864), Vol. I, p. 35.

[36] *Farington's Diary*, November 22, 1793.

[37] Mrs. Papendiek: *Court and Private Life in the Time of Queen Charlotte* (1887), Vol. II, p. 121.

[38] *Harcourt Papers*, Vol. XI, p. 109.

[39] *The Diary and Correspondence of Charles Abbot, Lord Colchester*, edited by Charles, Lord Colchester, Vol. II (1861), pp. 320–1. See also John Britton's *Architectural Antiquities of Great Britain* (1812), Vol. III, p. 37 *n.*

[40] *Horace Walpole's Correspondence*, Yale edn., Vol. II, p. 363.

[41] *Farington's Diary*, December 16, 1796, and November 6, 1797.

[42] Ibid., February 14 and June 8, 1794.

[43] Ibid., January 16, 1800.

[44] Ibid., January 12, 1794, and March 26, 1806.

[45] MS. diary of Mrs. Kennedy in the Royal Library.

[46] *Farington's Diary*, January 8, 1804.

[47] *Harcourt Papers*, Vol. VI, p. 83.

[48] *Windsor and Eton Express*, August 27, 1820.

[49] Ibid., August 6, 1823.

[50] Ibid., August 30 and September 22, 1823, and February 24, 1824.

[51] Ibid., July 19, 1825.

[52] *Journal of Mary Frampton* (1885), p. 337.

[53] Henry Ashton: *Illustrations of Windsor Castle by the late Sir Jeffry Wyatville, R.A.*, p. 2. The scholarly introduction to this work, by Ambrose Poynter, is the best source of information about Wyatville's alterations.

[54] *Gent. Mag.*, July 1805, p. 631, col. 2, foot.

[55] John Gore: *Creevey's Life and Times* (1937), p. 226.

[56] Royal Archives, Georgian Papers, 51308.

[57] Ibid., 27045.

[58] Royal Library: watercolour by G. H. Thomas.

[59] Ambrose Poynter, *loc. cit.*, p. 18.

[60] Royal Archives; Georgian Papers, 51343.

[61] Royal Archives; Georgian Papers, 24482.

[62] The bowling greens are shewn in Collier's plan dated 1742, reproduced in *Gent. Mag.*, April 1841, p. 372.

[63] *Windsor and Eton Express*, April 26, 1828.

[64] Ibid., September 6 and October 4, 1828. The fact that it was destined to become an orange garden was made known as early as the issue of August 12, 1826.

[65] Royal Archives, Addl. MSS., Georgian, Box 10, letter 99.

[66] John Gore, *op. cit.*, p. 307.

[67] Sir H. Lytton Bulwer: *Life of Lord Palmerston* (1870), Vol. I, p. 299.

PLATES

1. WINDSOR CASTLE, from St. Leonard's Hill.

2. THE NORTH FRONT FROM THE HOME PARK. The octagonal Brunswick Tower on the left was the creation of Wyatville, who lived in Winchester Tower at the extreme right. He also devised the two square towers in the centre in order to break up the plain front left by King Charles II.

3. THE LOWER WARD FROM THE WEST. On the left is St. George's Chapel, terminating in Master John Schorne's Tower (with the solid parapet): beyond this the "Albert Memorial" Chapel just shews. On the right are the Military Knights' lodgings, with the Round Tower in the background. At the top of the roadway the two low token walls mark the side of the ancient wall, ditch and gatehouse which until 1671 separated the Lower Ward from the Middle Ward.

4. THE UPPER WARD FROM THE SOUTH EAST. The view is taken from the Home Park. The corner tower in the centre was rebuilt in 1680 by Hugh May for King Charles II: its corbelled battlements were added by Wyatville. The small tower on the left of it, along the south front, is Augusta Tower. Then come the twin York and Lancaster Towers raised by Wyatville to flank the Long Walk, which enters the Quadrangle at this point. At the extreme left is the circular front of "King Edward III" Tower, built by King Henry III in 1223. The flagstaff marks the position of the Round Tower behind. The right-hand half of the photograph shows the east front.

5. THE EAST FRONT FROM THE SOUTH. In this march of towers along the east front the two centre ones were merely watch towers from about 1180, when they were built by King Henry II, until about 1360, when King Edward III added depth to them in order to provide living accommodation within: note the vertical line of white corner-stones half-way back along their depth. The wall across the foreground was built out by King George IV into the Home Park in order to enclose his new "sunk" garden.

6. THE NORTH TERRACE LOOKING WESTWARDS. In the foreground is the western end of Queen Elizabeth's Gallery, its archway dated 1583. The buttressed curtain wall beyond is of about 1180. The low tower in the wall is the Magazine Tower or Powder Mill, dated 1357. Beyond it rises Winchester Tower, rebuilt by William of Wykeham in the same year: it was restored by Wyatville, who inhabited it from 1824 until his death in 1840.

7. THE NORTH FRONT OF THE CANON'S CLOISTER. The two square towers nearest the camera are part of the original fortifications of King Henry II's curtain wall; the furthest one dates from King Edward III's foundation of the college. The Hundred Steps descend through the arch just visible at the foot of the centre tower.

8. THE EAST FRONT. Of about 1180 in date, but embellished with elaborate windows after King George IV had elected to adopt this wing as his residence. Between the wall-shrubs and the house runs the terrace walk added by King Charles II. The "sunk" garden on the left was added by King George IV: the steps in the foreground lead down to his orangery.

9. THE EAST TERRACE GARDEN. The marble vase, with bas-reliefs of the Judgement of Paris, is by Edward Pierce (d. 1698). One of Wyatville's less delicate windows appears behind.

10. THE APRON OR CHEMISE. This is the crenellated gallery at the top of William the Conqueror's mound. The Round Tower rises on the left, with the octagonal top of the Devil's Tower on the right.

11. WILLIAM THE CONQUEROR'S MOUND.

12. SUNDAY MORNING. Three Military Knights, in their uniform of scarlet and gold, disperse to their lodgings on the left after morning service. At the foot of the pavement is King Henry VIII's Gate.

13. KING HENRY VIII'S GATE. The pipes of the Irish Guards are emerging. This, the main entrance to the castle, gives access to the foot of the Lower Ward. First mentioned in 1194, it was rebuilt by King Henry VIII. It bears the pomegranate badge of Queen Catherine of Aragon, both over the arch and in a spandrel of a doorway within. Through the archway is seen the south flank of St. George's Chapel.

14. STATUE OF KING CHARLES II. This statue, cast in bronze by Josias Ibach in 1679, was commissioned by Tobias Rustat, a Page of the Backstairs to King Charles II. "The Horse at Windsor", wrote Wren in 1682, "was first cut in wood by a German, and then cast by one Ibeck, a founder, in London; but this is the dearer way." The Portland stone panels were carved by Grinling Gibbons.

15. THE QUADRANGLE or UPPER WARD looking westwards. The daily ceremony of the Changing of the Guard is in progress. The Round Tower stands on William the Conqueror's mound, with the Moat Path behind the wall at its foot, and the statue of King Charles II in front. The top half of the tower, from the heavy string-course upwards, is a collar of stone added by Wyatville for scenic effect. On the right is the State entrance, giving access to the State Apartments. The spectators beyond it owe their view of the proceedings to Wyatville's filling-in of the Conqueror's moat at the foot of the mound.

16. THE STATE ENTRANCE. This main entrance to the State Apartments was brought forward by Wyatville into the Quadrangle; its interior is shewn opposite. The statues of King Edward III (left) and the Black Prince are by Richard Westmacott. Two of King George III's windows in white Portland stone are shewn on the left; the remainder, in yellowish freestone, are by Wyatville.

17. THE QUEEN'S GUARD CHAMBER. Shewing the projection built out into the Quadrangle by Wyatville in order to form the State Entrance underneath; the exterior is shewn opposite. On the left, over a bust of the Duke of Marlborough, is the French banner rendered annually by the present Duke on the anniversary of the battle of Blenheim, as token rent for the royal park of Woodstock and the palace of Blenheim. The armour of the equestrian figure was worn by the King's Champion at the coronation of King George IV.

18. THE WEST FRONT. Shewing three of the drum towers of King Henry III, built in 1227–30, from the Curfew Tower at the far end to Salisbury Tower next the camera. The ancient masonry between the towers contrasts with those portions which were refaced when the street houses were cleared away in the mid-nineteenth century.

19. THE CURFEW TOWER. After its restoration by Salvin in 1863. Its present shell is an exterior cylinder built around the original wall within. The curtain wall on the right is ancient: note the transition from its pleasing irregularity of texture to the impeccable Victorian standard as it approaches the tower. Over the top appear the brick chimneys of the Horseshoe Cloister.

20. INTERIOR OF THE CURFEW TOWER. Shewing the massive oak staging erected to support the bell-cage when the ring of bells was transferred in 1478 from the former belfry in the Lower Ward. Note the steep and primitive staircase still in daily use by the attendant to John Davis' clock of 1689.

21. VAULTS OF THE CURFEW TOWER. Built in 1227 in the Norman ditch of the castle at its N.W. angle.

22. PORCH TO THE COLLEGE OF ST. GEORGE. Built in 1353 by Geoffrey Carlton, this was the normal entrance to the two cloisters of the College. Before St. George's Chapel was built (1478) priests returning from the Lower Ward, behind the camera, would enter this porch, turning to the right for their cloisters, or to the left for their other buildings in the area given them in 1409 by King Henry IV.

23. THE DEAN'S CLOISTER. Built in 1353 by King Edward III for the priests of his new College of St. George, who worshipped in the forerunner of the present "Albert Memorial" Chapel.

24. THE CANON'S CLOISTER. Looking eastwards, towards the Round Tower. Across the middle runs a passage leading from the Dean's Cloister on the right to the Hundred Steps on the left. These lodgings were built in 1353.

25. THE HORSESHOE CLOISTER. Seen through the doorway at the west end of St. George's Chapel. The tall gable behind is the back of the Curfew Tower. The brick and timber houses of the lay clerks are larger than they appear here to be because on the other side the ground falls steeply to the street. The noble and necessary stone steps in the foreground are unexpectedly modern: they were built by Sir G. Gilbert Scott in 1872, to replace a grassy mound.

26. THE "ALBERT MEMORIAL" CHAPEL. Begun in 1494 by King Henry VII as a tombhouse for King Henry VI and himself; abandoned by him, and also successively by Cardinal Wolsey and King Henry VIII. King George III formed a royal crypt beneath its floor; and Queen Victoria eventually dedicated it to the memory of her husband.

27. ST. GEORGE'S CHAPEL: BUTTRESSES AND BEASTS. This photograph, taken from the roof, shews the manner in which the outward thrust of the stone vault is communicated to low buttresses, and partly counterpoised by the King's Beasts. Originally these appear to have been all Tudor Dragons: but in the restoration of 1921–30 assorted Yorkist beasts were placed along the north flank of the chapel, and Lancastrian beasts along the south flank, in allusion to the tombs of Edward IV and Henry VI on either side of the altar below.

28. ST. GEORGE'S CHAPEL: THE EAST END. This triple arcade, which now forms the eastern end-wall of St. George's Chapel, was originally the West Front of the older chapel on the site of the "Albert Memorial" to-day. It dates from 1240. The pair of doors in the centre forms the subject of the illustration opposite. The tombstone in the floor, in the immediate foreground, is that of Sir Jeffry Wyatville, who died in 1840.

29. ST. GEORGE'S CHAPEL: THE DOORS OF THE EAST END. Formerly the entrance doors to King Henry III's chapel of 1240. The scroll-work in wrought iron is of exceptional quality; it is signed GILEBERTUS. The woodwork was originally covered with scarlet gesso.

30. THE NAVE FROM THE WEST END. The stone vault of the nave was finished in 1503: that of the choir ('more pendant and hollower') was begun in 1506. The process was completed in 1528 by King Henry VIII, who vaulted the crossing over the organ-loft. Below the upper windows is the choir of angels.

31. ST. GEORGE'S CHAPEL: THE SOUTH CHOIR AISLE. In the foreground is the tomb of King Edward VII and Queen Alexandra: in the next bay is that of King Henry VI. This was the corner of the building devised as the focal point for pilgrimages.

32. THE CHOIR FROM THE EAST END. St. George's Chapel is not the domestic chapel of the castle; it is specifically the chapel of the Order of the Garter, and this illustration shews the portion in which its ceremonial is observed. The Knights occupy the richly-canopied stalls; their banners hang above the crested helmets, and their enamelled plates are affixed to the backs of the stalls. The Sovereign's stall is on the left of the lectern, beside the entrance door. The tombstone in the centre of the floor marks the burial place of King Henry VIII with Queen Jane Seymour: the body of King Charles I occupies the same tomb.

33. THE VAULT OVER THE CROSSING. The central boss displays the arms of King Henry VIII and the date 1528. Of the four banners on the left-hand side, the nearest is that of The King, with The Queen's next to it.

34. THE ROYAL PEW. King Edward IV, the originator of St. George's Chapel, is buried behind the iron screen at bottom-right; and the two compartments above formed the chantry chapel in which masses were said for his soul. The right-hand oriel formerly resembled the stone one at top left, until King Henry VIII replaced it by the present wooden one, which bears the pomegranate badge of his first wife, Queen Catherine of Aragon. Since her time it has been known as the Royal Pew, although it is not normally used as such. The massive candlestick below is a replica of the four which were intended to stand by the tomb of King Henry VIII, but which are now in the church of St. Bavon in Ghent. This pair was presented by King George V and Queen Mary.

35. THE OXENBRIDGE CHANTRY. This chantry, in the southern aisle of the choir, corresponds with the Hastings chantry in the northern aisle: the two are similar, this being slightly the later in date since Canon John Oxenbridge, for the care of whose soul it was erected, did not die until 1522. In the spandrels over its door are carved in stone an Ox, an N, and a Bridge. Like the Hastings chantry, it contains a sequence of four paintings, recording the story of the beheading of St. John the Baptist: this bears the date 1522, and is in a more sophisticated style than the earlier one concerning St. Stephen.

36. VAULT OF THE KITCHEN PASSAGE. Built by John Martyn in 1362.

37. THE STATE ENTRANCE HALL. Built in 1362 by John Martyn. The State Entrance is off the picture in the left foreground. Guests pass down this hall, turning to the right at the end to ascend Salvin's Grand Staircase. The heavy bases to the columns shew where the floor has been lowered to give extra height.

38. THE QUEEN'S AUDIENCE CHAMBER. The painted ceiling by Antonio Verrio, which bears in each corner the cypher of King Charles II, dominates the whole and illustrates the pictorial quality of this Baroque style of architecture. It was the day of the artist, and the resplendent tapestries after J. F. de Troy drive the point home. Woven at the Gobelins manufactory between 1779 and 1785, these form a set of seven representations of the story of King Ahasuerus and Esther. The suite of gilt furniture of the period of King George I came from Stowe, and was presented in 1939 by Her Majesty the Queen.

39. THE QUEEN'S PRESENCE CHAMBER. This room is a longer version of the Audience Chamber through the door at the further end. It has the carved cornice which distinguishes all the rooms in the Star Building of King Charles II. Over the door is Kneller's portrait of Frances Stuart, Duchess of Richmond, who sat for the figure of Britannia on the penny. Over the fireplace is Elizabeth, Duchess of Orleans, with her children. The busts, by Roubiliac, represent Handel (in the corner) and Field-Marshal Lord Ligonier.

40. KING CHARLES II'S DINING ROOM. Over the mantelpiece is Queen Catherine of Braganza, painted by Jacob Huysmans in 1664. The carved frame by Grinling Gibbons is of unexcelled exuberance. On either side are tapestries displaying the arms of William and Mary; these, together with the pair of Queen Anne mirrors, were presented by Her Majesty Queen Mary. In the foreground is a terra-cotta bust of King Charles II.

41. THE STATE BEDROOM. At the foot of the state bed is the French eagle, and beneath it the initials of the Emperor Napoleon III and the Empress Eugenie, who occupied this room in 1855.

42. THE RUBENS ROOM. In former days the King's Drawing Room. On the left is King Philip II of Spain: over the fireplace the Holy Family: on the right St. Martin dividing his Cloak. The last named, by Van Dyck, is the only painting in the room not by Rubens.

43. THE WATERLOO CHAMBER. Formerly Horn Court, in the middle of the castle, it was roofed to house King George IV's collection of portraits by Sir Thomas Lawrence. The table is laid for dinner on Waterloo Day.

44. HOLBEIN PORTRAITS IN THE PICTURE GALLERY. In the bottom row are shewn Sir Henry Guildford, Master of the Horse (left), Derick Born, a merchant of the Steelyard, and Thomas Howard, 3rd Duke of Norfolk, as Earl Marshal.

45. THE CHILDREN OF KING HENRY VIII. Queen Mary Tudor on the left, King Edward VI at the top, and Queen Elizabeth on the right. In the centre is a portrait of Hans of Antwerp painted by Holbein in 1532, and given to King Charles I by Sir Henry Vane.

46. FIREPLACE IN THE GRAND RECEPTION ROOM. On the mantelpiece stands a chinoiserie clock from Brighton Pavilion.

47. THE GRAND RECEPTION ROOM. Decorated for King George IV in the French taste, and hung with Gobelins tapestries illustrating the story of Jason. Formerly the King's Guardchamber: visitors in those days would enter by the doorway half-way down on the right, having ascended from the interior courtyard known as Horn Court.

48. THE VAN DYCK ROOM. South-east corner. The picture of the five children of King Charles I was painted by Van Dyck for the King in 1637: their mother, Queen Henrietta Maria, is seen in the next picture. The painting nearest the camera shews Thomas Killigrew and Thomas Carew, two poets and playwrights at the court of King Charles I. The chandeliers of which one is seen here were commissioned in 1805 by King George III for this room to encourage English manufactures.

49. THE VAN DYCK ROOM. North-east corner. The Van Dyck paintings in this corner constitute a family party, representing the children of King Charles I and those of his chief minister, George Villiers, first Duke of Buckingham. Queen Henrietta Maria is in the corner, with three of her family on the right—Charles II, and Princess Mary (who became the mother of William III), and James II between them. The two lads and the larger lady, Duchess of Richmond, were the Villiers children, companions of the royal family in childhood.

50. CABINET OF QUEEN HENRIETTA MARIA. One of a pair of cabinets in the Van Dyck Room, inlaid in *arbor vitae*. The silver mounts bear the monogram of Queen Henrietta Maria.

1a. SILVER FURNITURE OF KING CHARLES II. Traditionally said to have been presented by the citizens of London. Reflected in the mirror is the triple portrait of King Charles I painted by Van Dyck in order that Bernini might execute a bust from it in Rome. The bust perished in a fire, but the painting has survived.

1b. SILVER FURNITURE OF KING WILLIAM III. This table and mirror are said to have been presented by the citizens of London to King William III and Queen Mary, whose monogram and arms they bear. The pineapple, which appears as a decorative motif under the table, had recently been introduced into England by the gardener of King Charles II. Reflected in the mirror is the painting by Van Dyck which appears in Plate 48.

52. QUEEN ELIZABETH'S GALLERY. Built by her as a cul-de-sac out of her bedroom (behind the camera). It was King William IV who first converted it into a library: there had not previously been one at Windsor—apart from the Green Drawing Room of King George IV, which was a library only in name.

53. FIREPLACE IN QUEEN ELIZABETH'S GALLERY. Described by St. John Hope as probably the finest example of its period in the kingdom. The inscription carved in the cornice states that it was built for the Queen in 1583, the 25th year of her reign and the 50th of her age. Along the lintel over the opening is an array of ten King's Beasts: the plain stone surround below this, and between the (original) carved pilasters, was inserted in 1932 in place of an unsightly one in red marble which dated only from 1834.

54. THE GRAND STAIRCASE. Visitors come up from the left, by the wheeled gun, before ascending the central staircase in the foreground. The armour of King Henry VIII is surmounted by Chantry's marble statue of King George IV.

55. ST. GEORGE'S HALL. The nearer end was King Charles II's domestic chapel, only the further end being originally St. George's Hall. Wyatville, who pulled down the dividing wall, was responsible for the present decorative scheme, including the modern shields of former Knights of the Garter along his new wooden ceiling.

56. THE GRAND CORRIDOR. Designed by Wyatville to link the private apartments which lie behind the wall on the right. Less than one third of its length is shewn here.

57. THE OAK DINING ROOM. Built by Wyatville over his new Sovereign's Entrance. Over the mantelpiece is the portrait of Queen Victoria aged 11, by her drawing-master, Richard Westall, R.A.

58. THE STAR CHAMBER. The panelling in this room came from the notorious Star Chamber in the Palace of Westminster which was dismantled in 1836.

59. THE SITTING ROOM OF H.M. THE QUEEN. Reflected in the mirror is the unfinished portrait by Gainsborough of Anne Luttrell, Duchess of Cumberland; she is seen with her husband (brother to King George III) in the oval painting by the same artist.

60. THE GREEN DRAWING ROOM. The curtained window looks out over the East Terrace towards London.

61. THE GREEN DRAWING ROOM. With a portrait of Princess Sophia by Sir Thomas Lawrence.

62. THE CRIMSON DRAWING ROOM. Shewing a pair of the suite of doors brought by King George IV from Carlton House.

63. THE WHITE DRAWING ROOM.

64. THE DRIVE TO ASCOT.

LIST OF TEXT ILLUSTRATIONS
AND
LIST OF PLATES

LIST OF TEXT ILLUSTRATIONS

LIST OF PLATES